THE MEGATASTIC KIDS' JOKE BOOK

THE MEGATASTIC KIDS' JOKE BOOK

ARCTURUS

ARCTURUS

This edition published in 2009 by Arcturus Publishing Limited
26/27 Bickels Yard, 151–153 Bermondsey Street,
London SE1 3HA

ISBN: 978-1-84837-391-4
CH001287EN

Printed in the UK

Contents...

TEACHER, TEACHER

Why did the maths teacher take a ruler in his car?

So he could see how long it took him to get to work in the morning!

I hope you aren't going to spend the whole lesson watching the clock!

Certainly not, Sir, I have my alarm set for 3.45, and I'm hoping to get a little nap later!

What do you shout when Santa Claus does the register?

Present!

I thought you were going to play
school with me today!

I did – I decided to play absent!

✎

What do you do if someone faints in a
maths exam?

Try to bring them 2!

✎

Parent – Why have you given my little boy such a bad
report – he's as intelligent as the next boy!

Teacher – Yes, but the next boy is an idiot!

✎

Why are you taking that sponge into your lesson?

I always find History such an absorbing subject!

✎

Did you hear about the maths teacher who
was thrown out of the pizza restaurant –
for asking how long his pizza would be?

Vicar – Can anyone tell me what Samson did for a living ?

**Pupil – I think he was a comedian -
it says in the Bible that he
brought the house down !**

Why does your teacher have her hair in a bun ?

Because she has a face like a burger !

Why do teachers never marry dairy farmers ?

They are like chalk and cheese !

Why do doctors enjoy their schooldays ?

Because they are good at examinations !

So, Blenkinsop, you claim to know all your tables –
let's hear them then !

Dining Room table, Kitchen table, Living Room table........

COLLECTIVE NOUNS....

A NUMBER of maths teachers !

A RANGE of cookery teachers !

A TEAM of P.E. teachers !

A CONCENTRATION of science teachers !

A BAND of music teachers !

A FOREST of woodwork teachers !

A BANK of economics teachers !

A SCHOOL of headteachers !

Teacher – Sally, give me a sentence with the word aroma in it !

Sally – My uncle Fred is always travelling, he's aroma !

What did the ghostly music teacher play ?

Haunting melodies !

Why do vampire teachers not like computers ?

They hate anything new fangled !

The maths teacher is feeling run down today !

Wow ! Did anyone get the number of the car that did it !

What happens to a maths teacher's class when he retires ?

Before or after you've woken them up ?

LET ME INTRODUCE THE FAMILY...

The maths teacher's son – Juan !

The music teacher's daughters – Melody and Carol !

The woodwork teacher's daughter – Giselle !

The caretaker's daughter – Mona !

The computer teacher's son – Chip !

✎

Now – just settle down you lot !
I don't come into this classroom to
listen to this sort of racket !

Oh – where do you usually go, Miss ?

✎

What is the plural of mouse ?

Mice !

What is the plural of house ?

Hice !

My maths teacher is a real peach !

You mean she's pretty ?

No – I mean she has a heart of stone !

Teacher – I'd like a ticket to Cambridge please !

Travel Agent – Single sir ?

Teacher – No, actually I'm married to Miss Whelk the
Chemistry teacher !

We can't possibly play football out there –
the pitch is wet through !

**I know – the first years have been doing
dribbling practise all morning !**

John – what is the plural of baby ?

Twins !

In the Bible it tells us that God was a healer !

I know that, Sir, because he gave Moses some tablets !

If you multiply 245 by 3456 and divide the answer by 165, then subtract 752, what will you get ?

The wrong answer, Miss !

Blenkinsop, what do birds eat for their breakfast ?

Tweet - a - bix !

What's the difference between a train and a teacher ?

A train says "choo - choo" but a teacher says "take that gum out of your mouth this instant !"

Why did the scruffy schoolboy finally take a bath ?

Because he realised that grime doesn't pay !

Blenkinsop - your parents are multi-millionaires, and yet you still smell awful !

That's because we're filthy rich, Miss !

Inspector - How many teachers work in this school ?

Pupil - Very few !

How do you make a sick insect better ?

Give it a T, then it will be a stick insect !

What do history teachers do before they get married ?

They go out on dates !

Who teaches all the boys called Ed ?

The Ed teacher !

I didn't use a recipe for this casserole -
I made it out of my own head !

I thought it tasted of sawdust !

What's the difference between a school and
a headmaster's car?

One breaks up and the other breaks down !

Why are you always late for school ?

Because I threw my alarm clock in the bin !

Why on earth did you do that ?

**It kept going off when I was still asleep
and waking me up !**

❀

Where do vampire schoolchildren go for field trips ?

Lake Eerie !

❀

Why are you scratching yourself boy ?

Because no-one else knows where I itch !

❀

Blenkinsop, where is Turkey ?

No idea, Sir, we threw ours away after Christmas !

❀

IT teacher – Smith give me an example of software ?

Smith – a floppy hat !

I think our school must be haunted – because teacher keeps going on about the school spirit !

Blenkinsop, are you any good at History ?

Well, Miss, to be honest, yes and no !

What do you mean yes and no ?

I mean, yes, I'm no good at History !

Why were you late this morning Veronica ?

Veronica – I squeezed the toothpaste too hard and it took me half an hour to get it all back into the tube again !

Blenkinsop – if I were to borrow £100 from your father, and he paid me back at a rate of £10 per month, how much would he owe me after 6 months ?

£100, Sir !

Oh, dear, Blenkinsop, I'm afraid you don't know much about maths do you ?

And you don't know much about my father !

✎

Violin for sale – going cheap – no strings attached !

✎

Why did the teacher pick Snodgrass to be teacher's pet ?

Because he is the person who looks most like her dog !

✎

What has 22 legs, is dripping wet and sings out of tune ?

The school football team in the showers after a match !

What sort of vampire is attracted to music and soldiers?

A sharp major!

How many millions of times have I told you, Blenkinsop, stop exaggerating!

Why did the music teacher ban skeletons from keyboard lessons?

They have no organs!

Why is that boy locked up in a cage in the corner of the classroom?

Oh, he's the teacher's pet!

This school pie has hairs in it!

That's odd – it says rabbit pie on the menu!

There once was a schoolboy called Pete,
Who stuck coloured pens on his feet.
Now where ever he goes,
If he wiggles his toes,
He can draw, on the floor – now that's neat !

Rodrick, how would you address a Dutchman
and his twin brother ?

In double Dutch, Miss !

My little Ben is doing so well at school –
he can speak 3 languages fluently –

**Double Dutch, complete twaddle and
utter gibberish !**

What do you get if you look at a vampire
teacher through a telescope ?

A horrorscope !

A bottle of lemonade went to teacher training college. He
wanted to teach fizzical education !

Why was the teacher chased by a hen?

It was after his wages – he said he got paid chicken feed!

How does a maths teacher remove hard wax from his ears?

He works it out with his pencil!

You've been playing with that blotting paper the whole lesson –

You obviously find it very absorbing!

Blenkinsop, name five things that contain milk !

Yogurt, cheese, and 3 cows !

My Brian is very quick at picking up music –
they always send for him when they want
to move the school piano !

Now, for your Art homework I want you to
draw a self portrait !

Does it matter who it's a portrait of, Miss ?

How did people react when electricity was
first discovered ?

They got a nasty shock !

How did people react when gas was first used
to heat homes ?

**Most people were happy, but one or two people
were a bit sniffy about it !**

How does the robot teacher get out of the
school at home time ?

He makes a bolt for it !

✎

What does the robot teacher's *mum* do
for a living ?

She's a washer woman !

✎

How can you tell when a robot teacher
is going mad ?

He goes screwy !

✎

Please French teacher,
Listen to me,
I don't know the French,
But I really need a Oui !

✎

**Did you hear about the music teacher who kept
forgetting her register !?**

Why did the music teacher tell his pupil to beat it ?

He was teaching him to play the bass drum !

What sort of music makes a teacher take
his shoes off ?

Soul music !

What do you call a satellite that
takes secret pictures ?

An unidentified spying object !

Is the maths teacher in a good mood today ?

I wouldn't count on it !

Teacher – Who can tell me which sea creature eats
its prey two at a time ?

Pupil – Naoh's shark !

How do you make the school loudmouth

into the football team coach ?

**Easy, just pull out his teeth and put 11 seats
in his mouth !**

Did you hear about the ex maths teacher
who worked on the stock exchange ?

**He was divided about whether to buy
additional shares or take away his profits !**

What class did the new robot teacher get on
his first day ?

He got all the nuts !

One in three people are stupid – so have a good look at two of your classmates.

If they seem OK, then it's probably you!

I always come out in spots when I'm doing a maths exam!

Sounds like a bad case of decimals!

I sprained my ankle and had to miss games for 2 weeks!

Lucky you! Our sports teacher never accepts a lame excuse for missing games!

The school dinners here are untouched by human hand – there's a gorilla in the kitchen!

Our school dinners are full of iron – which is probably why they are so difficult to chew!

Our school kitchens are spotlessly clean –
which is why the food always tastes of soap !

I couldn't do my homework
last night because my pen
ran out, and I'm not allowed
to go out of the house
after dark !

Blenkinsop, what is the covering
of a tree trunk called ?

Don't know, Sir !

Bark, Blenkinsop, Bark !

Woof, woof !

It's a good job your name is Mark –

**Because you certainly don't seem able to get
any in your exams !**

Did you hear about the Spanish teacher who broke his leg, but was back at work 2 hours later ?

He made a maracas recovery !

When did early people start wearing clothes ?

In the Iron Age !

Sir, what would I have to write to get 3 'A' levels ?

Someone else's name at the top of your exam paper !

Why did 1920s gangsters in America carry musical instrument cases ?

Because they committed robbery with violins !

Mr Blenkinsop, I really think your daughter needs an encyclopaedia for school !

Why can't she walk like all her friends ?

What happens to children at magic school
who misbehave ?

They are ex - spelled !

Smith – why weren't you here at 8.45 this morning ?

Because I was held up by that sign outside – it says 'stop children crossing'!

We're doing Byron in English class !

What was he famous for ?

I think he invented the ball point pen !

Turn on the TV quick and you'll be able to see our school photograph!

Why, are they doing a programme about your school?

No, it's Crimewatch!

If we do the 10 times table, 10 times, how many times will we have done it?

Is it a trick question?

Did you hear about the school cleaner who married a history teacher?

He was brushing up some old dates and he swept her off her feet!

Joe - how can you work out the age of a tree monkey?

Cut it in half and count the rings?

You had better behave in Mr Simkins' music class or you'll find yourself in treble !

Good morning class – said the vampire English teacher –

– today we will learn the alphabat !

The teachers have been working flat out in the staffroom, marking exam papers !

Really – I thought they were asleep as usual !

What qualifications do I need to be a pantomime horse ?

Three neigh levels !

Smith – how do you feel about H G Wells ?

No, idea, Sir, we get all our water from a tap !

How can a school cook also be a history teacher?

**Easy – if they know more than anyone else
about ancient grease!**

FOR SALE – MUSIC TEACHER RETIRING

One piano complete with stool, sheet music,
and earplugs!

Why did Catherine of Aragon marry Henry VIII?

**She was told she needed a ruler to help her
with her maths exam!**

Blenkinsop – why haven't you learned your times table ?

Because we get the Guardian, Miss !

Where would I find Offa's Dyke ?

I think you should be asking Offa that question, Miss, not me !

Do you think my son has what it takes to be a pilot ?

Well – he certainly spends plenty of time with his head in the clouds !

What happens to old maths teachers ?

They are taken away !

What happens to old history teachers ?

They reach their best before date !

What happens to old music teachers?

They send in a note!

What happens to old french teachers?

One day they realise that un ouef is enough!

Does your father still help you with your homework?

No, Miss, I can get it wrong all on my own now!

The Deputy Head is a funny chap,
who creeps from class to class.
He has a face that could curdle cream
and a voice like broken glass.

Why does this class keep shouting Miss, Miss, Miss when you know very well that your teacher is a married woman ?

Because she keeps dodging the stuff we throw at her !

Well, son, how did you find your geography exam ?

With a map and compass, how else !

Smith – if I gave you £5 a week for the next 6 months what would you have ?

An insane teacher !

Apple crumble – my favourite !

Well, it was apple pie until the cook dropped it on the floor and the crust shattered !

Today is flying saucer day in school dinners –

because we get unidentified frying objects !

Did you hear about the science teacher who was always playing tricks on people ?

He was a real particle joker !

Did you hear about the geography teacher who mapped out his career ?

Or the archaeology teacher whose job was in ruins ?

Head – You'll start on a salary of £15,000 and then go up to £20,000 in six months time.

Teacher – In that case I think I would like to start in six months time !

Blenkinsop, I think you need glasses !

What makes you think that, Sir ?

You're facing the wrong way !

Lewis – what do you get if you drop a
piano down a mineshaft ?

A flat minor !

Blenkinsop, how many times have I told you
not to eat sweets in class ?

Six, Miss !

Rather more than six I think, young man !

Yes, but that's as far as I can count !

If you want to test the theory about a link between television and violence - try telling your maths teacher that you sat and watched television all night instead of doing your homework !

Did you hear about he school head who gave a pupil some lines for the first time in his career ?

It was head line news !

Sir, have you ever hunted bear ?

No, Blenkinsop, but I've been fishing in a pair of swimming trunks !

Does anyone know why the Romans built straight roads?

Yes, Sir, because they didn't have steering wheels on their chariots !

Blenkinsop – How would you discover what life in Ancient Egypt was really like ?

Blenkinsop – I'd ask my Mummy !

What do you call an assistant headteacher who thinks he's a cowboy ?

The Deputy Head !

Why do history teachers like fruit cake ?

Because it's full of dates !

Why did the teacher leave his job ?

He was head hunted !

Susie, How do you make a milk shake ?

Take it to a scary film, Miss !

You, boy, which part of a fish weighs the most ?

The scales, sir !

Do your pupils miss you ?

No, that's why I've got this bruise on my forehead !

What musical instrument does the school cat play ?

A Mouse organ !

What sort of insect plays music ?

A Humbug !

Why are school singing classes like someone locked out of his house ?

Because neither of them can find the right key !

To get a job as head of geography you need abroad knowledge of the subject !

SCHOOL LIBRARY - NEW BOOKS

The Haunted House
by
Hugo First !

The Broken Window
by
Eva Brickatit

The Filthy Chinese Farmhouse
by
Who Flung Dung !

The Hungry Man
by
Edna Breakfast !

Today we are going to look for the lowest common denominator...

Haven't they found that yet, my dad says they were looking for that when he was at school !

Blenkinsop – you deserve a hundred lines for this homework !

Ah, but it wouldn't be fair on the rest of the class if I always got what I deserved would it, sir !

Teacher – who discovered Pluto ?

Pupil – Walt Disney !

Parent – Do you think my son will make a good
Arctic explorer ?

**Teacher – I would think so, most of his
marks are below zero !**

Please don't talk while you are doing your exam !

It's alright, miss, we're not doing the exam – just talking !

Pupil – Ugh! There's a fly in my soup !

**Kitchen assistant – Don't worry, the spider on your
bread will get it !**

Science teacher – Name two liquids that don't freeze...

Mary – Coffee and tea !

Why are maths teachers no good at gardening ?

Because everything they plant grows square roots !

Did you hear about the maths teacher whose mistakes
started to multiply ?

They took him away in the end !

History teacher – Who shot King Harold ?

Blenkinsop – My mum told me never to tell tales !

Where do crazy teachers train?

Loony - versity!

Where do alien teachers train?

Moony - versity!

Did you hear about the stupid
P.E. teacher?

He was a physical jerk!

Blenkinsop, do you understand how important
punctuation is?

Yes, Miss, I always make sure I get to school on time!

Head – what do you think about in the school holidays?

Pupil – I never think about schoolwork!

Head – Not really much of a change for you then!

Wendy, when do you like school the best?

During the school holidays, Sir!

Brian, what is water?

A colourless liquid which turns black when I put my hands in it!

What do Atilla the Hun and Winnie the Pooh have in common?

The!

What do skeleton teachers say at the start of the lesson?

As there is nobody here we can start!

Smith, name me someone who has been round the globe?

Terminator, Miss!

Who on earth is Terminator?

My goldfish!

Watson, shouldn't you wash your hands before you start your piano lesson ?

No, Miss, I only play on the black notes !

Carol, what is the difference between a policeman and a soldier ?

You can't dip a policeman into your boiled egg, Sir !

Why are you putting in those ear plugs ?

I've got to teach form 4B tennis, and they always make such a racket !

What is a good pet for small children ?

A Rattle snake !

Teacher – Blenkinsop – Give me a sentence with the word detention in it !

Blenkinsop – I had to leave the horror film before it had finished, because I couldn't stand detention !

5 GOOD REASONS TO GO TO SCHOOL

1. Even school dinners are better than my mum's.

2. The heating goes off at home at 9 o'clock.

3. You learn to be independent – by not doing as you are told.

4. The video shop doesn't open 'til 4 o'clock

5. You learn what life will be like when you are old and grumpy – by watching the teachers at coffee break.

Teacher – Mary, why was no-one able to play cards on Noah's Ark ?

Mary – Because Noah stood on the deck !

Now, Roger, if a half-filled barrel of beer fell on someone, how badly hurt would they be?

Not at all if it was light ale, Miss!

Now, can anyone tell me what Egyptian Kings were buried with?

Yes, Miss, they were buried with their *Nammaforrs*!

What is a *Nammaforr*?

Knocking nails in!

Blenkinsop, how can
you prove that the
Earth is round ?

I didn't say it was, Sir !

What do you call a
teacher swearing ?

A Sir - Cuss !

For tonight's homework I want you to write an
essay on a goldfish.

I can't do that Sir !

Why on earth not ?

I don't have any waterproof ink !

Head Master – Mr Snurge, Why have you put the school
orchestra into the freezer ?

**Mr Snurge – They said they wanted to play some
music that was a little more cool !**

What is the difference between frogspawn
and school pudding ?

Frogspawn was once warm !

How can you tell if a teacher is in a good mood ?

Let me know if you ever find out !

Why are you always late for school ?

**It's not my fault, you always ring the bell before
I get here !**

I'm not really interested in maths – I just go along to the
lesson to make up the numbers !

Sir, can we do some work on the Iron Age today?

Well, I'm not certain, I'm a bit rusty on that period of history!

Why did Cyclops have to retire from teaching?

He only had one pupil!

Why is your homework late, Bloggs?

Sorry, Miss, my Dad is a slow writer!

Smith, How would you hire a horse?

Put a brick under each leg?

Did you hear about the teacher who went
to a mind reader ?

She gave him his money back !

Blenkinsop, how do you get rid of varnish ?

Just take out the 'R', Miss !

Harry, what does it mean if I say
'Guten Morgen Herr Dresser' ?

It means you've gone for a haircut !

Smith, where do fish sleep ?

On a waterbed !

Sally, what musical instrument do Spanish
fishermen play ?

Cast - a - nets !

Bill, which is heavier, a full moon or a half moon ?

A half moon, because a full moon is lighter !

Mary, how did you find the questions
in your English exam ?

**Oh, I found the questions easily enough, it's the
answers I couldn't find !**

Geoff, why are you eating with a knife ?

Because my fork leaks !

Who invented fractions?

Henry the eighth!

Ten cats were at the cinema. One walked out.
How many were left?

None - they were all copycats!

Wally, what is a dumb waiter?

Someone who gets all the orders mixed up, Sir!

Sue, describe crude oil for me!

**Well, Sir, it is black and sticky and it floats on the
surface of water shouting 'knickers'!**

Teacher – Smith, what were people wearing during the Great Fire of London?

Smith – Blazers, smoking jackets and hose!

✎

Where did the metalwork teacher meet his wife?

In a bar!

✎

What happened after the wheel was first invented?

It caused a revolution!

✎

Robert, why do doctors and nurses wear masks in the operating theatre?

So no-one will know who did it if they make a mistake!

✎

How do archaeologists get into locked tombs?

Do they use a skeleton key, Miss?

Steven, why did Henry the eighth have so many wives ?

He liked to chop and change, Miss ?

DID YOU HEAR ABOUT ...

The P.E. teacher who used to run around the exam room in the hopes of jogging pupils memories ?

The maths teacher and the art teacher who used to go out together painting by numbers ?

The craft teacher who used to have the class in stitches ?

The science teacher who was scared of little glass dishes – he was petrified ?

The cookery teacher who thought Hamlet was an omelette served with bacon ?

Why did the school canteen hire a dentist ?

To make more filling meals !

Sarah, where would you find a gorilla ?

In a kitchen ?

Jane, what do you know about the Dead Sea ?

I didn't even know it had been poorly, Sir !

William, what is a fungi ?

A mushroom that likes having a good time ?

'John can't come to school today,
because he has a cold.'

'Who am I speaking to ?'

'My father.'

Harry, spell mouse trap...

C. A. T. !

Billy, what is a wombat ?

It's what you use to play Wom, Miss !

What exams do farmyard animals take ?

Hay levels !

Carol, can you give me a sentence with deliberate in it ?

'My dad bought a new settee and tomorrow they are going to deliberate to our house !'

What do you call the teacher who
organises all the exams ?

Mark !

Blenkinsop, I do wish you would pay a little attention !

I'm paying as little as I can, Sir !

Why were ancient sailing ships more eco-friendly ?

**Because they could go for hundreds of miles
to the galleon !**

Howard, which is the largest sea ?

The Galax-sea !

Fred, how do fleas get from one animal to another ?

They itch hike !

Gloria, did you write this poem all by yourself ?

Yes, Miss !

Well, well, and I thought Shakespeare was a man !

John, what is the longest word in the
English dictionary ?

Elastic !

How do you work that out ?

It stretches !

James, give me a sentence with the word
fascinate in it !

**Fatty Perkins' coat has ten buttons, but he can
only fascinate of them !**

Howard, if I had 12 sausages in one hand, and 15 sausages in the other, how many sausages would I have altogether?

No idea, Miss, I'm a vegetarian!

✑

Freda will make a good astronomer when she leaves school, as she is very good at staring into space for hours on end!

✑

What makes you think that my son, Martin, is always playing truant?

Martin? There's no Martin in this school!

What do you call a man who keeps on talking when no-one is listening?

Sir!

I hope I don't catch you cheating in the maths exam!

So do I, Miss!

Fred, what food do giraffes eat?

Neck - tarines!

Mary, why have you brought that fish into school?

Because we will be practising scales in the music lesson!

Teacher – John, name me a famous religious warrior?

John – Atilla the Nun!

Philip, why do you always have two plates
of food for school dinner ?

It's important to have a balanced diet, Miss !

Mandy, do you have to come to school chewing gum ?

No, Sir, I can stay at home and chew it if your prefer !

Teacher – Did you know that most accidents
happen in the kitchen ?

Pupil – Yes sir, but we still have to eat them !

Teacher – Steven, what's a computer byte?

Steven – I didn't even know they had teeth!

Where were traitors beheaded?

Just above the shoulders!

Graham, what are net profits?

What fishermen have left after paying the crew!

William, how do you make a Mexican chilli?

Take him to the South Pole, Miss!

Mum – Do you say a little prayer before you
eat your school dinner?

Son – Good heavens no – the food isn't that bad!

George, you have had a very undistinguished career at this
school – have you ever been first in anything?

Only the lunch queue, Miss!

Why is the school cheese on toast hairy?

**Because the cook dropped it on the floor
then wiped it on her jumper!**

How can bats fly without bumping into anything?

They use their wing mirrors!

Sarah, give me a sentence with the word illegal in it!

My dad took me to the bird hospital the other day and we saw a sick sparrow and an illegal!

William, how fast does light travel?

I don't know, Sir, it's already arrived by the time I wake up!

What do you give a sick bird?

Tweetment!

How many maths teachers can you get in an empty Mini?

Just one - after that it isn't empty any more!

Miriam, what is the hottest planet in our solar system?

Mer - Curry!

Time to get up and go to school!

I don't want to go! Everyone hates me and I get bullied!

But you have to go - you're the headteacher!

Teacher - Sarah - what evidence is there that smoking is harmful to the health?

Sarah - well look what happened to all the dragons!

Teacher: Millie, why do you say that Moses wore a wig?

Millie: Because sometimes he was seen with Aaron, and sometimes without !

✎

ANIMAL SCHOOL REPORTS

Cheetah - A nice enough boy but not to be trusted..

Leopard - Has missed a lot of classes this year due to spots.

Hyena - Seem sto think that everything is a joke.

Stick insect - Never been the same since the elephant mistook him for a pencil !

✎

Teacher - Why were you late for school today Carol ?

Carol - I got a flat tyre on my bicycle !

Teacher - Did you run over some broken glass ?

Carol - No Sir, there was a fork on the road !

Pupil – Those eggs look a bit past their best !

School Cook – Don't blame me, I only laid the tables !

✎

What do you call an American cartoonist ?

Yankee Doodle !

✎

Blenkinsop, you could be in the school football team,
if it weren't for two things !

What are they, Sir ?

Your feet !

BLENKINSOP'S FEET !

73

In South America, cowboys chase cattle
on horseback !

WOW ! I didn't know cows could ride at all !

Who was the fastest runner of all time ?

Adam, because he was first in the human race !

My dad baked some cakes, and said I have to
give one to my teacher !

Gee ! I never realised just how much he
must hate your teacher !

You have a photographic memory Blenkinsop. Its a shame
that nothing ever develops !

TEACHER, TEACHER

Blenkinsop – Why do birds fly south in the winter ?

Because it is too far to walk !

What is a snake's favourite subject ?

Hissss-tory !

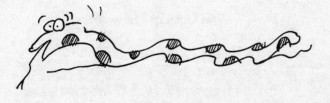

Teacher – Jarvis, tell me a sentence with the word
counterfeit in it.

**Jarvis – I wasn't sure if she was a centipede or a
millipede so I had to count her feet !**

What's the difference between a bird watcher
and a teenager ?

**One gets a hide and spots, the other gets
a spot and hides !**

What does an elf do after school ?

Gnome work !

✎

You have to be a really good whistler to use the school toilets here !

Why is that ?

The locks are all broken !

✎

If I cut a potato in two, I have two halves.
If I cut a potato in four, I have four quarters.
What do I have if I cut a potato in sixteen ?

Chips !

How did knights make chain mail?

From steel wool?

Why did the flea get thrown out of school?

He just wasn't up to scratch!

Why was the glow worm sad?

Because her children weren't very bright!

In this examination you will be allowed
15 minutes for each question !

Crikey, they sound like long questions !

What did the music teacher need a ladder for ?

Reaching the top notes !

Your son will be a good printer's assistant !

What makes you say that ?

He's exactly the right type !

Did you have any problems with your
French on your school trip to Paris?

No, but the French certainly did!

Terry, how do you join the Police Force?

Handcuff them together?

John, name one use of Beech wood!

Making deck chairs?

What is easy to get into, but
difficult to get out of ?

Trouble !

What was the blackbird doing in the school library ?

My mum says the school beef pie is good for you because
it is full of iron !

That explains why it's so tough then !

What was the blackbird doing in the school library ?

Looking for bookworms !

Mary, what do you think a pair of
crocodile shoes would cost?

**That would depend on the size of your
crocodile's feet Miss!**

Fred, I told you to write 100 lines because your
handwriting is so bad, but you have only done 75!

**Sorry Miss, but my maths is just as
bad as my handwriting!**

Jim, what is 'won't' short for ?

Will not, Miss !

Very good. What is 'don't' short for ?

Er...Donut Miss ?

Harry, how would you fix a short circuit ?

Add some more wire to make it longer, Sir ?

I banged my head on the locker door this morning !

Have you seen the school nurse ?

No, just stars !

Where do dim witches go ?

Spelling classes !

Well, Geoff, did you get a good position in the
maths test yesterday ?

**Yes, Sir, I was in front of a radiator, and next to
the smartest person in the class !**

Teacher – *Name a bird that doesn't build its own nest ?*

Pupil – *The Cuckoo*

Teacher – *That's right ! How on earth did you know that ?*

Pupil – Everyone knows that Cuckoos live in clocks !

Do you know a boy called Jim Wibley ?

Yes, he sleeps next to me in Geography !

Michael, can you name two inventions that have helped mankind to get up in the world ?

... Yes, Miss, the stepladder and the alarm clock !

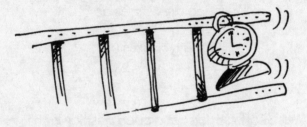

What do you call it when the Headteacher doesn't tell the truth about nits in his hair ?

Head Lice !

How many teachers work at your new school Sam ?

About half of them !

Why was the teacher's head eleven inches long ?

Because if it was twelve inches it would be a foot !

Blenkinsop – Sir, my parents want me to tell you that they were really pleased with my last report

Teacher – But I said you were a complete idiot !

Blenkinsop – But it's the first time anyone in our family has been really good at something !

You shouldn't play those notes on the piano !

Why not ?

You'll get into treble if you do !

Caroline, how many days of the week start
with the letter 'T' ?

**Four: Tuesday,
Thursday,
Today and
Tomorrow !**

THE SCHOOL NOTICE BOARD

Violin for sale – really cheap – no strings attached !

Dog free to good home – eats anything.
Loves children !

Why did the school orchestra have such
awful manners ?

Because it didn't know how to conduct itself !

What comes out of a teacher's wallet
at 100 miles an hour ?

Stirling Moth !

**Table for sale, by Mr Wibley
with wooden legs !**

On the school field trip a crab bit my toe!

Which one?

I don't know, all crabs look the same to me!

We love our school, we really do.
We love our lessons, teachers too!

We love the exams and the tricky tests.
We love the school dinners and the P.E. vests!

But why do I sound so cheerful today?
Because we just started the summer holiday!!

KNOCK, KNOCK...

Knock, Knock !
Who's there ?
Justin
Justin who ?
Justin time to let me in !

Knock, Knock !
Who's there ?
Anna
Anna who ?
Anna noying habit of yours – locking the door like this !

Knock, Knock !
Who's there ?
Josie
Josie who ?
Josie anyone else out here ?

Knock, Knock !
Who's there ?
Paula
Paula who ?
Paula door open and you'll see !

Knock, Knock !
Who's there ?
Annette
Annette who ?
Annette Curtain !

Knock, Knock !
Who's there ?
Angus
Angus who ?
Angus me coat up and put the kettle on !

Knock, Knock !
Who's there ?
Oasis
Oasis who ?
Oasis, its your brother. I forgot me key !

Knock, Knock !
Who's there ?
Alma
Alma who ?
Alma time seems to be spent on this doorstep !

Knock, Knock !
Who's there ?
Zeke
Zeke who ?
Zeke and you will find out !

Knock, Knock !
Who's there ?
Phil
Phil who ?
Phil this cup with sugar would you, I've run out !

Knock, Knock !
Who's there ?
Frank
Frank who ?
Frank you for asking !

Knock, Knock !
Who's there ?
Homer
Homer who ?
Homer goodness, I've come to the wrong house !

Knock, Knock !
Who's there ?
Alex
Alex who ?
Alex the way you've done the garden !

Knock, Knock !
Who's there ?
Chas
Chas who ?
**Chas pass the key through the letter box and
I'll open the door myself !**

Knock, Knock !
Who's there ?
Mo
Mo who ?
Mo than you'll ever know !

Knock, Knock !
Who's there ?
Matt
Matt who ?
**Matt as well settle down, looks like I'm in
for a long wait !**

Knock, Knock !
Who's there ?
Dana
Dana who ?
Dana nice day out here, hurry up and let me in !

Knock, Knock !
Who's there ?
A. Lister
A. Lister who ?
A. Lister good reasons why you should open the door !

Knock, Knock !
Who's there ?
Zeb
Zeb who ?
**Zeb better be a good reason for keeping
me waiting out here !**

Knock, Knock !
Who's there ?
Greta
Greta who ?
**Greta friend like that again, and you'll end
up with none at all !**

Knock, Knock !
Who's there ?
Egon
Egon who ?
Egon down the shops !

Knock, Knock !
Who's there ?
Will
Will who ?
Will I have to wait much longer ?

Knock, Knock !
Who's there ?
Woody
Woody who ?
Woody open the door if we asked him nicely ?

Knock, Knock !
Who's there ?
Kline
Kline who ?
Kline of you to invite me round !

Knock, Knock !
Who's there ?
Polly
Polly who ?
Polly door handle again, I think it's just stiff !

Knock, Knock !
Who's there ?
Keith
Keith who ?
Keith your hands where I can see them !

Knock, Knock !
Who's there ?
Imogen
Imogen who ?
Imogen you were out here...

Knock, Knock !
Who's there ?
India
India who ?
India is some of my stuff, and I've come to collect it !

Knock, Knock !
Who's there ?
Kat
Kat who ?
Kat you again ?

Knock, Knock !
Who's there ?
Al Gore
Al Gore who ?
Al Gore to the window so you can see me !

Knock, Knock !
Who's there ?
Alvin
Alvin who ?
Alvin your heart – just you vait and see !

Knock, Knock !
Who's there ?
Tom
Tom who ?
Tom to the window and have a look !

Knock, Knock !
Who's there ?
Candy
Candy who ?
Candy owner of this big red car come and
move it off my drive !

Knock, Knock !
Who's there ?
Alfie
Alfie who ?
Alfie good to see you again!

Knock, Knock !
Who's there ?
Kim
Kim who ?
Kim just too late to see you !

Knock, Knock !
Who's there ?
Adair
Adair who ?
Adair you to guess !

Knock, Knock !
Who's there ?
Chuck
Chuck who ?
Chuck the key under the door and I'll let myself in !

Knock, Knock !
Who's there ?
Khan
Khan who ?
Khan you give me a lift to school ?

Knock, Knock !
Who's there ?
Mavis
Mavis who ?
Mavis be the last time you keep me waiting !

Knock, Knock !
Who's there ?
Darren
Darren who ?
Darren nother excuse to keep me out here !

Knock, Knock !
Who's there ?
Luke
Luke who ?
Luke through the letterflap and you'll see !

Knock, Knock !
Who's there ?
Colin
Colin who ?
Colin in for a chat !

Knock, Knock !
Who's there ?
Wendy
Wendy who ?
Wendy you want me to call round again ?

Knock, Knock !
Who's there ?
Tori
Tori who ?
Tori - I got the wrong address !

Knock, Knock !
Who's there ?
Trudy
Trudy who ?
Trudy my word I've come to collect you !

Knock, Knock !
Who's there ?
Trish
Trish who ?
Bless you !

Knock, Knock !
Who's there ?
Cameron
Cameron who ?
Cameron say that !

Knock, Knock !
Who's there ?
I Know Kung fu
I Know Kung fu who ?
I'd better not upset you then !

Knock, Knock !
Who's there ?
Cohen
Cohen who ?
Cohen to knock just once more, then I'm going away !

Knock, Knock !
Who's there ?
Kent
Kent who ?
Kent you stop asking questions and open the door !

Knock, Knock !
Who's there ?
Alan
Alan who ?
Alan 'nounce myself once you've opened the door ! !

Knock, Knock !
Who's there ?
Penny
Penny who ?
Penny for the guy mister ?!

Knock, Knock !
Who's there ?
Postman
Postman who ?
Just the postman with your letters - you're thinking of
Doctor Who !

Knock, Knock !
Who's there ?
Ahmed
Ahmed who ?
Ahmed a big mistake coming here didn't I ?!

Knock, Knock !
Who's there ?
Ginger
Ginger who ?
Ginger hear the doorbell ?

Knock, Knock !
Who's there ?
Courtney
Courtney who ?
Courtney door, can you open it and let me loose ?

Knock, Knock !
Who's there ?
Isabell
Isabell who ?
Isabell not working ?

Knock, Knock !
Who's there ?
Eeny Minnie
Eeny Minnie who ?
Eeny Minnie Miny Mo !

Knock, Knock !
Who's there ?
Guess Simon
Guess Simon who ?
Guess Simon the wrong doorstep !

Knock, Knock !
Who's there ?
Cattle
Cattle who ?
**Cattle get out if you open the door,
I'll come in through teh window !**

Knock, Knock !
Who's there ?
Wendy
Wendy who ?
Wendy come to collect the rent, I'm off !

Knock, Knock !
Who's there ?
Amos
Amos who ?
Amos quito is chasing me – please let me in !

Knock, Knock !
Who's there ?
Arnie
Arnie who ?
Arnie ever going to let me in ?!

Knock, Knock !
Who's there ?
Ken
Ken who ?
Ken you come out to play ?

Knock, Knock !
Who's there ?
Sid
Sid who ?
**Sid you'd be ready to go at three –
what's gone wrong !**

Knock, Knock !
Who's there ?
Seymour
Seymour who ?
Seymour of me by opening the door !

Knock, Knock !
Who's there ?
Sid
Sid who ?
Sid down and I'll explain !

Knock, Knock !
Who's there ?
Charlie
Charlie who ?
Charlie you know the sound of my voice by now !

Knock, Knock !
Who's there ?
Hedda
Hedda who ?
Hedda nough of this – I'm off !

Knock, Knock!
Who's there?
Ivan
Ivan who?
Ivan idea you're going to keep me waiting out here!

Knock, Knock!
Who's there?
Gin
Gin who?
Gin know how cold it is out here!

Knock, Knock!
Who's there?
Farmer
Farmer who?
Farmer distance your house looks much bigger!

Knock, Knock !
Who's there ?
Linda
Linda who ?
Linda hand to get this heavy suitcase up the steps !

Knock, Knock !
Who's there ?
Tex
Tex who ?
Tex you ages to open the door !

Knock, Knock !
Who's there ?
Hardy
Hardy who ?
Hardy har, fooled you !

Knock, Knock !
Who's there ?
Yul
Yul who ?
Yul soon see !

Knock, Knock !
Who's there ?
Courtney
Courtney who ?
Courtney good football matches lately !

Knock, Knock !
Who's there ?
Mary
Mary who ?
Mary Christmas, ho, ho, ho !

Knock, Knock !
Who's there ?
Mickey
Mickey who ?
Mickey don't fit - have you changed the lock ? !

Knock, Knock !
Who's there ?
Jester
Jesterwho ?
Jester minute I've forgotten !

Knock, Knock !
Who's there ?
Giraffe
Giraffe who ?
Giraffe to ask me that stupid question ?

Knock, Knock !
Who's there ?
Harry
Harry who ?
Harry up and let me in !

Knock, Knock !
Who's there ?
Ringo
Ringo who ?
Ringo, ringo roses... !

Knock, Knock!
Who's there?
Mike
Mike who?
Mike your mind up!

Knock, Knock!
Who's there?
Spock
Spock who?
**Spock the difference between me
and my twin brother!**

Knock, Knock!
Who's there?
Teacher
Teacher who?
Teacher self for a few days, I'm off on my hols!

Knock, Knock !
Who's there ?
Tessa
Tessa who ?
Tessa long time for you to open the door !

Knock, Knock !
Who's there ?
Carl
Carl who ?
**Carl round to my house and I won't
keep you waiting !**

Knock, Knock !
Who's there ?
You
You who ?
Hello !

Knock, Knock !
Who's there ?
Simon
Simon who ?
Simon every occasion - you always make me wait !

Knock, Knock !
Who's there ?
Princess
Princess who ?
Princess not to come round here any more !

Knock, Knock !
Who's there ?
Morgan
Morgan who ?
Morgan you could ever imagine !

Knock, Knock !
Who's there ?
Jacqueline
Jacqueline who ?
Jacqueline Hyde !!

Knock, Knock !
Who's there ?
Callista
Callista who ?
Callista warm reception I was expecting !

Knock, Knock !
Who's there ?
Teresa
Teresa who ?
Teresa jolly good fellow !

Knock, Knock !
Who's there ?
Mouse
Mouse who ?
Mouse get a key of my own !

Knock, Knock !
Who's there ?
Batman
Batman who ?
You mean there's more than one ?!

Knock, Knock!
Who's there?
Caine
Caine who?
Caine you see me through the glass!

Knock, Knock!
Who's there?
Egbert
Egbert who?
Egbert no bacon!

Knock, Knock!
Who's there?
Misty
Misty who?
Misty door bell again!

Knock, Knock!
Who's there?
Lester
Lester who?
Lester worry about!

Knock, Knock !
Who's there ?
Just Paul
Just Paul who ?
Just Pauling your leg - it's Steve really !

Knock, Knock !
Who's there ?
Fitz
Fitz who ?
**Fitz not too much trouble -
can you please open the door !**

Knock, Knock !
Who's there ?
Major
Major who ?
Major mind up to open the door yet ?

Knock, Knock !
Who's there ?
Mandy
Mandy who ?
Mandy lifeboats !

Knock, Knock !
Who's there ?
Belle
Belle who ?
Belle don't work, so I'm having to knock !

Knock, Knock !
Who's there ?
Alex
Alex who ?
Alex to knock on doors and run away

Knock, Knock !
Who's there ?
Kent
Kent who ?
Kent you fix the doorbell ! ?

Knock, Knock !
Who's there ?
Vance
Vance who ?
Vance more I knock on your door in the dead of night !

Knock, Knock !
Who's there ?
Yootha
Yootha who ?
Yootha person with the second hand cooker for sale ?

Knock, Knock !
Who's there ?
Ozzie
Ozzie who ?
Ozzie you still have the same front door
you did the last time I called !

Knock, Knock !
Who's there ?
Chester
Chester who ?
Chester minute – I'm in the wrong street !

Knock, Knock !
Who's there ?
Carl
Carl who ?
Carl this a friendly greeting - 'cos I don't !

Knock, Knock !
Who's there ?
Mustapha
Mustapha who ?
Mustapha good reason to keep me waiting !

Knock, Knock !
Who's there ?
Willy
Willy who ?
Willy hurry up and let me in !

Knock, Knock !
Who's there ?
Posh
Posh who ?
Posh the door open and you'll see !

Knock, Knock !
Who's there ?
Baby
Baby who ?
Baby I shouldn't hab come round wiv dis cold !

Knock, Knock !
Who's there ?
Fred
Fred who ?
Fred you'll have to let me in !

Knock, Knock !
Who's there ?
Russell
Russell who ?
**Russell up a nice hot cup of tea -
it's freezing out here !**

Knock, Knock !
Who's there ?
Midas
Midas who ?
Midas well open the door and find out !

Knock, Knock !
Who's there ?
Bart
Bart who ?
Bart time you opened this door !

Knock, Knock !
Who's there ?
Denise
Denise who ?
Denise are cold - let me in !

Knock, Knock !
Who's there ?
May
May who ?
May I come in ?

Knock, Knock !
Who's there ?
Lass
Lass who ?
How long have you been a cowboy ?

Knock, Knock !
Who's there ?
Doctor
Doctor who ?
**No, Doctor Smith – you sent for me
because you have a cold !**

Knock, Knock !
Who's there ?
Norbut
Norbut who ?
Norbut a lad !

Knock, Knock !
Who's there ?
Giselle
Giselle who ?
Giselle flowers in there ?

Knock, Knock !
Who's there ?
Will
Will who ?
Will wait out here until you let us in !

Knock, Knock !
Who's there ?
Jaffa
Jaffa who ?
Jaffa keep me waiting ?

Knock, Knock !
Who's there ?
Posy
Posy who ?
Posy open the door and find out ?

Knock, Knock !
Who's there ?
Terminator
Terminator who ?
**Terminator sandwiches early, so she sent
me to get some more !**

Knock, Knock !
Who's there ?
Yul
Yul who ?
Yuletide greetings neighbour !

Knock, Knock !
Who's there ?
Walter
Walter who ?
Walter strange thing to ask !

Knock, Knock !
Who's there ?
Wade
Wade who ?
Wade a minute I'll just check !

Knock, Knock !
Who's there ?
Jerome
Jerome who ?
Jerome at last !

Knock, Knock !
Who's there ?
Karl
Karl who ?
Karl again another day !

Knock, Knock !
Who's there ?
Vince
Vince who ?
Vince some time since I saw you last !

Knock, Knock !
Who's there ?
Donna
Donna who ?
Donna expect you to remember me !

Knock, Knock !
Who's there ?
Red
Red who ?
Red your letters, you can have them back now !

Knock, Knock !
Who's there ?
Pearce
Pearce who ?
Pearce this balloon with a pin !

Knock, Knock !
Who's there ?
Jools
Jools who ?
Jools like these should be worth a lot of money !

Knock, Knock !
Who's there ?
Whoo ooo oooo ooo
Whoo ooo oooo ooo who ?
Ah, good, this is the ghosts club !

Knock, Knock !
Who's there ?
Fletch
Fletch who ?
**Fletch a bucket of water,
your house is on fire !**

Knock, Knock !
Who's there ?
Icing
Icing who ?
**Icing carols –
you give me money !**

Knock, Knock !
Who's there ?
Alf
Alf who ?
Alf feed the cat while you're on holiday !

Knock, Knock !
Who's there ?
Jethro
Jethro who ?
Jethro this at me ?

Knock, Knock !
Who's there ?
Nona
Nona who ?
Nona your business?

Knock, Knock !
Who's there ?
Stephanie
Stephanie who ?
Stephanie me - who else could it be !

Knock, Knock !
Who's there ?
Dan
Dan who ?
Dan just stand there - let me in !

Knock, Knock !
Who's there ?
Lefty
Lefty who ?
Lefty home on your own again !

Knock, Knock !
Who's there ?
Orang
Orang who ?
Orang the doorbell but it doesn't seem to work, so now I'm knocking !

Knock, Knock !
Who's there ?
Arthur
Arthur who ?
Arthur minute and I'll show you my identification !

Knock, Knock !
Who's there ?
Mickey
Mickey who ?
Mickey fell down the drain, can you give me a lift ?

Knock, Knock !
Who's there ?
Mayor
Mayor who ?
Mayor come in ?

Knock, Knock !
Who's there ?
Butcher
Butcher who ?
Butcher said I could come and visit you !

Knock, Knock !
Who's there ?
Greengrocer
Greengrocer who ?
Greengrocer rushes oh !

Knock, Knock !
Who's there ?
Al
Al who ?
Al huff and I'll puff and blow your house down !

Knock, Knock !
Who's there ?
Howard
Howard who ?
Howard you know if you won't even open the door ?

Knock, Knock !
Who's there ?
Elvis
Elvis who ?
Elvis is a complete waste of time. I'm off !

Knock, Knock !
Who's there ?
Olly
Olly who ?
Olly need is love !

Knock, Knock !
Who's there ?
Ant
Ant who ?
Ant I told you already !

Knock, Knock !
Who's there ?
Colin
Colin who ?
Colin round to see you !

✐

Knock, Knock !
Who's there ?
Lucinda
Lucinda who ?
Lucinda sky with diamonds... !

✐

Knock, Knock !
Who's there ?
Jester
Jester who ?
Jester day, all my troubles seemed so far away... !

✐

Knock, Knock !
Who's there ?
Our Tell
Our Tell who ?
Our Tell you what I want, what I really really want...!

Knock, Knock !
Who's there ?
Honor Claire
Honor Claire who ?
Honor Claire day, you can see forever...!

Knock, Knock !
Who's there ?
Carrie
Carrie who ?
Carrie your bags to the airport for a fiver ?

Knock, Knock !
Who's there ?
Avon
Avon who ?
Avon to trink your blood !

Knock, Knock !
Who's there ?
Otto
Otto who ?
Ottold you not two seconds ago !

Knock, Knock !
Who's there ?
Carter
Carter who ?
Carter stray dog - is it yours ?

✎

Knock, Knock !
Who's there ?
Woody
Woody who ?
Woody lend me a tenner till payday ?

✎

Knock, Knock !
Who's there ?
Europe
Europe who ?
Europe bright and early today !

✎

Knock, Knock !
Who's there ?
Wallace
Wallace who ?
Wallace is a fine how do you do...!

Knock, Knock !
Who's there ?
Othello
Othello who ?
Othello could freeze to death out here !

Knock, Knock !
Who's there ?
Kong
Kong who ?
Kongratulations you've won the lottery !

Knock, Knock !
Who's there ?
Toodle
Toodle who ?
Where are you going – I only just got here !

Knock, Knock !
Who's there ?
Superman
Superman who ?
You know I can't reveal my secret identiity !

GHOSTLY GOINGS-ON

Should baby monsters eat humans on an empty stomach ?

No, they should eat them on a plate like everyone else !

✏

How do monsters write letters?

With fountain men !

✏

Why do monster mums and dads tell their children to eat cabbage ?

Because they want them to have a healthy green complexion !

✏

Why did the ghost get the job ?

Because he was clearly superior !

✏

Did you hear about the giant monster who took
a hump-back in a plastic box to
work with him ?

It was his packed hunch !

What did the monster get when he fell
through a window ?

A pane !

What do they sing in the vampire version of Abba ?

Fang you for the music !

Why did the zombie go to the chemist ?

He wanted something to help stop his coffin !

What is the first thing you should put into a
haunted house ?

Someone else !

What do they employ in monster hospitals ?

A skeleton staff !

Baby Monster – When I grow up I want to drive a tank !

**Mummy Monster – Well, I certainly won't
stand in your way !**

✏

Why was the monster called porridge ?

Because he was grey and thick !

✏

What should you do after shaking hands
with a monster ?

Count your fingers !

✏

What is a monster's favourite game ?

Squash !

✏

Did you hear about the zombie who was having a party –
he didn't know how many people would be coming – it
would depend on who he could dig up !

What did the blacksmith do when he saw
Frankenstein's neck ?

He made a bolt for it !

How did the fruit bats go into Noah's Ark ?

In pears !

Did the computerised monster have any brothers ?

No, but he had hundreds of tran - sisters !

How did you know I was a ghost ?

Oh, I can see right through you !

When a vampire drinks too much, what does he get ?

A Fangover !

Why do vampires go to lots of pop concerts ?

They love being in fang clubs !

What did King Tut-Ankh-Amun hate most of all ?

Having to go shopping with his mummy !

Why was the mummy covered in gold and silver shiny bandages with big bows ?

It was his Christmas wrapping !

Did you hear about the mummy who wanted
to be a rock star ?

He started his own rock bandage !

What do ghostly policemen do ?

They haunt down criminals !

What sort of monsters work in graveyards ?

A skeleton staff !

Did you hear about the werewolf who
dropped his trousers ?

Well - it was a full moon !

How do you scare vampires ?

Ask if they would like a little garlic with their steak !

How does a vampire lock his coffin ?

With skeleton keys !

Did you hear about the overweight cannibal from Sweden ?

He was always eating swedes between meals !

How do monsters eat their dinner ?

They wolf it down !

VAMPIRE SAYINGS

A neck in your hand is worth two in a bush !

A stitch in time – means I can come back for some more !

There's many a slip twixt neck and lip !

Why did one skeleton tell the other one off?

Because he had been telling fibulas!

What sort of monster lives in your hanky?

A bogeyman!

What sort of monster drinks tinned blood?

A Canpire!

VAMPIRE HUNTERS MENU

GARLIC BREAD

followed by

HAMMERED STEAK

followed by

HOT CROSS BUNS

Hurry up, said the father skeleton to his son, or you'll be late for the skull bus !

Why does the monster shop at the sewage works ?

He likes convenience food !

What is the first thing a monster eats in a restaurant ?

The waiter !

What do vampires eat for lunch ?

Fangers and mash !

What did the monster say when he threw a human into a pit of werewolves ?

Looks like you're going to the dogs !

Why is the tribe of Bolog now extinct ?

Because monsters used to eat lots of spagetti with Bolog knees !

Where did the vampire go on his holiday in China ?

Fang - Hi !

Why are vampires good at treating people with coughs and colds ?

Because they can clear your throat in seconds !

Which monster is the most untidy ?

The Loch Mess Monster !

Why is monster coffee so noisy ?

Because they like scream in it !

What is the shortest and nastiest party game that monsters know ?

Swallow the leader !

Why do monsters make good fashion models ?

Because no matter what they are wearing they always look so ghoul !

What does a monster call knights in armour ?

Tinned food !

What do you call a pair of ghostly glasses?

Spectre - calls!

What do you take to a vampire party?

The girl necks door!

How did the ghostly teacher make sure his pupils had learned what he had written on the blackboard?

He went through it again!

What do monsters eat for a light meal?

Light bulbs!

Why did the monster buy an axe !

Because he wanted to get a-head in life !

How do two monsters decide who
owns something ?

They fright each other for it !

How do vampires try out a new blood group ?

They suck it and see !

How do vampires get clean ?

In a blood bath !

Did you hear about the ghost who
cut down trees at three o'clock
in the morning ?

He was the thing that made stumps in the night !

What noise do baby witches make when
they are playing with toy cars ?

Broom, Broom !

What is a ghost's favourite film ?

The Deer Haunter !

Why was the stone monster always short of money ?

He was always hard up !

What do you call a kind, helpful monster who likes flowers
and butterflies ?

A Failure !

What fictional character are werewolves afraid of ?

Long John Silver !

Who do vampires invite to their weddings?

All their blood relatives!

Why do ghosts never feel guilty?

They have a clear conscience!

What do you call a vampire that you can dip
into your tea?

Count Dunkula!

Why was the monster catching centipedes?

He wanted scrambled legs for breakfast!

Why do vampires never invite trolls to their dinner parties ?

They can't stand all that goblin !

Ꙫ

What tennis players do monsters like to eat ?

Bjorn on the cob !

Ꙫ

What did the vampire do when someone accused him of drinking blood ?

He didn't bat an eyelid !

Ꙫ

Why should you never invite monsters to a housewarming party ?

Because they bring flame throwers !

Ꙫ

What game do ghostly mice play at parties ?

Hide and Squeak !

Where would you find a suitable gift for a
tortured ghost ?

In a chain store !

I see Dracula has a new job –
he's a cashier in a blood bank !

You know that a barking vampire dog never bites....

....but when it stops barking, you better run !

What is visible – invisible – visible – invisible –
visible – invisible ?

A skeleton on a zebra crossing !

How do vampires show affection for each other ?

They bat their eyelids !

What do you call a hairy monster that's lost ?

A where-am-I wolf !

What do you call an escaped hairy monster ?

A where's-he-gone wolf !

What is Frankenstein's worst nightmare ?

Being nude in a room full of people – without a stitch on !

What is the difference between a ghost and a custard cream bisuit ?

Have you tried dipping a ghost in your tea ?!

When Mr Dracula put on his coat one evening his wife asked if he was going to the pub with his friends.

No, dear, he replied. Just popping out for a bite !

What is a ghost's car called ?

Squeals on wheels !

What does Dracula drink ?

De-coffinated - coffee !

What do you get if you put a monster on your roof ?

A bite on the tiles !

What does Dracula have fitted to the front of his car?

Head vamps!

Which monster ate the three bears?

Ghouldilocks!

What did Dracula say when someone said his teeth were ugly?

I'll fang you not to say that!

What sort of view do you get from the top of a pyramid?

As Pharaoh the eye can see!

What would you be if your daddy was a mummy and you were musical?

A wrap singer!

What is a monster's favourite TV soap?

Beastenders!

A vampire started acting very strangely, and
a passer-by asked if he was going mad –
the vampire replied that he was perfectly
sane, but just felt a little batty!

Did you hear about the monster who
fell asleep in an empty coffin?

It was a grave mistake!

My husband always looks a mess whenever there's a full
moon –

He's really going to the dogs!

Did you hear about the vampire burglar who was caught
red handed?

They caught him fang to rights!

What pets does Dracula own?

A Blood Hound and A Ghoul Fish!

Why do vampires have a steady nerve?

They are as ghoul as cucumbers!

Why do zombies always look so tired?

They are dead on their feet!

Where do vampires get washed?

In the bat room!

Why did Dracula advertise for a housekeeper ?

He wanted some new blood in the house !

Did you hear about the monster who went into a restaurant and ordered crocodile and chips ?

He was in a hurry so he shouted, "and make it snappy !"

If you're good at writing, Dracula has a job for you...

...he's looking for someone to answer his fang mail,

...and take on the job as his crypt writer !

How do you get a message to a deep sea monster ?

Drop him a line !

Why is the sea monster wet ?

Because the seaweed !

How do you know what a deep sea monster looks like ?

He's the one with the wavy hair !

How do you know if a monster fancies you ?

He'll roll his eyes at you !

And what should you do if that happens ?

Roll them back before someone steps on them !

In the monster version of the story of Snow White,
what are the seven dwarves called ?

Snacks !

Why do vampires avoid arguments ?

They hate to get cross !

Ō

What do you call a ghost that doesn't
scare anymore ?

A failure !

Ō

The monster went to his doctor and complained
of a split personality.

**Do sit down, the doctor said, and begin
by telling me which one of you is paying !**

Ō

"I think I need new glasses," said the
short-sighted monster.

"You certainly do," replied the dentist !

Ō

Who do you telephone to rent a Dracula costume ?

Vamp - hire !

How do you know if you had a drunken
vampire at your party ?

There are fang marks on the ketchup bottle !

What did Frankenstein do when the monster's head kept
falling off ?

He made a bolt for it !

What do you get if you cross a vampire with a robot ?

Something new fangled !

What about the two ghosts that got married –
it was love a tfirst fright !

Oh, red eyed vampire in the night,

you nearly gave my heart a fright.

All black and shiny, glistening red,

from pongy toes to slithery head.

If you had hoped to drink my blood,

and hoped that it would do you good,

I think you made a big mistake,

'cos I'd just been out for a steak!

Why did Dracula want to keep his baby teeth
for all eternity?

Because a fang of beauty is a joy forever!

166

Which window cleaners do vampires use ?

The one in pane - sylvania !

Why do monsters like to stand in a ring ?

They love being part of a vicious circle !

What do you call a ghostly teddy bear ?

Winnie the OOOoooooOooooohhHHhhhhh !

Why was the vampires bank account
always in the red ?

Because it was in a blood bank !

Why did the vampire go to the blood donor centre ?

To get lunch !

What do you call a Welsh ghost ?

Dai !

What do you call a tough Welsh ghost that stars in an action movie ?

Dai Hard !

Why did the England cricket team consult a vampire ?

They wanted to put some bite into the opening bats !

How do vampires start a duel?

They stand Drac to Drac!

When do ghosts wear red jackets and ride horses?

When they go out fox haunting!

Why are owls so brave at night?

Because they don't give a hoot for ghosts, monsters or vampires!

What did the old vampire say when he broke his teeth ?

Fangs for the memory !

Why do vampires holiday at the seaside ?

They love to be near the ghostguard stations !

What can yu use to flatten a ghost ?

A spirit level !

What do you call a dentist who really likes vampires ?

An extractor fan !

What do you call a
futuristic android
who comes back in
time to plant seeds ?

Germinator !

And what do you
call his twin brother ?

Germinator II !

What do you call the ghost of the handkerchief ?

The Bogie man !

What sort of wolf can you wear ?

A wear wolf !

Who delivers Christmas presents to werewolves?

Santa Claws !

What do you call a lazy skeleton ?

Bone Idle !

What do you call a ghostly would-be Scottish King ?

Boney Prince Charlie !

Why do ghosts catch cold so easily ?

They get chilled to the marrow !

What do you call a scary, boney creature that
staggers around making strange wailing noises ?

A supermodel making a record !

Why do ghosts go back to the same place every year for
their holidays ?

They like their old haunts best !

What should you say when a vampire
gives you a present ?

Fang you very much !

How do you know when there is a horrible
monster under your bed ?

You don't – that's what makes it so very scary !

Where in America do monsters go for their holidays?

Death Valley!

What do monsters like to pour on their
Sunday dinner?

Grave-y!

What do you call a ghostly haircut with long
curly strands of hair?

Deadlocks!

What do ghosts like
with their food?

A little whine!

What sport do monsters
like best?

Sculling!

What film is about a scary train robber ?

Ghost Buster !

Where do ghosts live ?

In flats !

Where do vampires like to go for their holidays ?

The Dead Sea !

Why did the two vampire bats get married ?

Because they were heels over heads in love !

WHAT GHOST'S WATCH ON TV

Scare Trek !
Horror Nation Street !
Bone and Away !
The Booos at Ten !
Sesame Sheet !
Have I got whooos For You !

What did the pirate get when he smashed
a skeleton up in a fight ?

A skull and very cross bones !

GHASTLY GHOSTLY SAYINGS

Never kick a ghost while he's down -
your foot will just go through him !

He who laughs last - obviously hasn't
seen the ghost standing behind him !

What do you call a young
skeleton in a cap and uniform ?

A skullboy !

Why did the skeleton fall into a hole?

It was a grave mistake!

What villain does the spooky 007 fight?

Ghoulfinger!

Why are hyenas always falling out?

They always have a bone to pick with each other!

Who delivers Christmas presents to vampires?

Sack-ula!

What vampire can you wear to protect
you from the rain ?

Mac - ula !

What is the fairy tale about a girl who
falls in love with a really ugly loaf of bread ?

Beauty and the yeast !

When they got married, what sort of children
did they have ?

Bun-shees !

Why did Goldilocks go to Egypt ?

She wanted to see the mummy bear !

AND, SPEAKING OF MUMMIES...

Mummy, mummy, what is a vampire ?

Be quiet and eat your soup before it clots !

Mummy, mummy, what is a werewolf ?

Be quiet and comb your face !

Mummy, mummy
I don't like my
uncle Fred !

**Well, just leave
him on the side
of your plate
and eat
the chips !**

Mummy, mummy I don't want to go to America !

Be quiet and keep swimming !

What should you wear when you go out
for a drink with a vampire ?

A metal collar !

What do you call a young woman who hunts vampires ?

A Miss Stake !

What do the police call it when they
watch a vampire's house ?

A stake out !

What do skeletons learn about at school ?

Decimals and fractures !

Why didn't the skeleton fight the monster ?

He didn't have the guts !

Ø

What did the ghostly show jumper always score ?

A clear round !

Ø

What does a young boy ghost do to get a girlfriend ?

He wooooooooooos her !

Ø

What did the young ghost call his mum and dad ?

His trans-parents !

Ø

Why don't you have
to worry what you
say to the werewolf
computer engineer ?

**His bark is worse
than his byte !**

What sort of jokes do werewolves like best ?

Howlers !

What happens when a werewolf meets a vampire ?

He doesn't turn a hair !

Why wasn't the werewolf allowed to get
off the lunar spaceship ?

Because the moon was full !

What room must all werewolf homes have ?

A changing room !

Why did the werewolf steal underwear
when the moon was full ?

**Because his doctor told him a change
was as good as a vest !**

What sort of news do werewolves fear ?

Silver bulletins !

Why did the shy werewolf hide in a cupboard
every full moon ?

Because he didn't like anyone to see him changing !

What did the train driver say to the werewolf?

Keep the change!

What form of self defence do werewolves use?

Coyote!

How do mummies knock on doors?

They wrap as hard as they can!

Why was the mummy done up in brightly coloured sparkly paper?

He was gift-wrapped!

What does it say on the *mummy's* garage entrance ?

Toot, and come in !

What do mummies use to fasten things together ?

A Hammer and Niles !

What do children in Egypt call their parents ?

Mummy and Daddy of course !

Why was the Egyptian Prince worried ?

Because his mummy and daddy were both mummies !

What do mummies shout when they are on a
sinking boat ?

A bandage ship !

What do mummies do to relax ?

They just unwind a little !

Why was the mummy's leg stiff ?

Because someone had been winding him up !

What did the ghost of the owl say ?

Too-wit too-wooooooooooooo....

Why are mummies good
at keeping secrets?

**They can keep things
under wraps for centuries!**

What are the scariest
dinosaurs?

Terror dactyls!

Why was the monster
hanging around the pond
with a net?

**He was collecting the
ingredients for toad in
the hole!**

Why is Godzilla sitting on a
friend like leaving home?

**Because you end up with a
flat mate!**

Who was the winner of the headless horse race?

No-one, they all finished neck and neck!

What did the President of the USA say to the giant ape when he won the lottery?

Kong - ratulations!

SKELEMENU...

Ox-Tail Soup

followed by

Spare Ribs and Finger Buffet

finishing with

Marrowbone Jelly and Custard!

What eats your letters when you post them?

A ghost box!

What spook delivers your letters?

Ghostman Pat and his skeleton cat!

Which creature saves people from drowning?

The Ghostguard!

Why did the vampire like eating chewy sweets?

He liked something to get his teeth into!

Why do sausages and bacon spit when
they are being cooked?

Because it's a terror frying experience!

189

What is the scariest thing you could find in
your Christmas stocking?

The ghost of Christmas presents!

Why did the vampire put tomato ketchup
on his sandwiches?

He was a vegetarian!

How do you grow a werewolf from a seed?

Just use plenty of fur-tiliser!

What do ghosts carry their luggage in
when they go on holiday?

Body bags!

Why can you never get through to a vampire
bat on the telephone?

Because they always hang up!

~

What do monsters eat at tea time?

Scream cakes!

~

Which vampire likes playing practical jokes?

Dracu-lark!

~

Where do vampires keep their savings?

In the blood bank!

What sort of voice do werewolves have ?

Husky ones !

What pop group did the young mummies join ?

A boy bandage !

What would you call a mummified cat ?

A first aid kit !

Why was Dracula ill
after biting someone
on a train home
from work ?

**He caught a
commuter virus !**

If hairy palms is the first sign of turning into
a monster, what is the second?

Looking for them!

How do you stop a werewolf attacking you?

Throw a stick for it to fetch!

What was on the haunted aeroplane?

An air ghostess and a lot of high spirits!

What do you call a vampire mummy?

Wrapula!

Why couldn't the ghost get a whisky
in the pub after 11 o'clock?

**Because they aren't allowed to serve
spirits after closing time!**

Why did the witch take her small
book of magic on holiday?

The doctor told her to get away for a little spell!

Who was the fattest mummy ever?

Two ton Carmen!

Why couldn't the witch's victim move?

He was spellbound!

Â°

What sort of horses do monsters ride?

Night mares!

Â°

What do sea monsters eat?

Fish and ships!

Â°

How does a skeleton know when it's going to rain?

He just gets a feeling in his bones!

Why do sea monsters go to so many parties?

They like to have a whale of a time!

Which sea monster rules the waves?

The Cod-father!

What do baby sea monsters play with?

Doll-fins!

Why was the vampire lying dead on the
floor of the restaurant?

It was a steak house!

What do you give a monster that feels sick?

Plenty of room!

Where do monsters sleep?

Anywhere they want to!

What do you get if a monster falls over in a car park?

Traffic jam!

What would you get if you combined a monster,
a vampire, a werewolf and a ghost?

As far away as possible!

What do monsters call a crowded swimming pool ?

Soup !

What do you get if you shoot a werewolf
with a silver bullet ?

A very interesting rug !

What do you call the ghost of a werewolf that
lives at the seaside ?

A Clear - Pier - Were - Wolf !

How did Frankenstein's monster escape from
the police ?

He made a bolt for it !

Why did Dracula visit a psychiatrist ?

He thought he was going batty !

What sort of music do vampires and ghosts like best ?

Haunted House Music !

If a monster buys you a chair for your birthday
should you accept it ?

Yes - but don't let him plug it in !

What does a monster shout when it is scared ?

Mummy !

Can you stick vampires to your window ?

Yes - they are suckers !

Why did the ghost go to the bicycle shop ?

He needed some new spooks for his front wheel !

What sort of jobs do spooks like ?

Dead end jobs !

Why did the monster have twins in his lunchbox ?

In case he fancied seconds !

Who do vampires invite to their birthday parties ?

Anybody they can dig up !

What do ghosts do if they are afraid ?

Hide under a sheet !

Why don't ghosts go out during the day ?

They are scared of people !

❦

Why don't skeletons have glass eyes ?

Because they come out in conversation !

❦

Why are vampires always cheerful ?

Because they are terrified of being cross !

❦

What is a werewolf's favourite film ?

Claws !

What do you get if you cross a vampire with
a knight of the round table ?

A Bite in shining armour !

What was Dr Frankenstein best at ?

Making new friends !

What do spooks eat in the morning ?

A hearty breakfast of Dreaded Wheat !

What has fifty legs ?

A centipede cut in half !

Why didn't the vampire laugh at the joke
about the wooden stake ?

He didn't get the point !

What do you get if you cross the Abominable
Snowman and Count Dracula ?

Severe frostbite !

Where do spooks go shopping ?

In BOOOO-tiques !

Where do Italian monsters eat ?

Spook - getti !

Why did the ghoul take so long
to finish his newspaper ?

He wasn't very hungry !

Why did the monster eat a settee and two
armchairs ?

He had developed a suite tooth !

MONSTERS FAVOURITE HOLIDAY DESTINATIONS

Eat a lee !
Belch um
Gnaw Wayne
Sweet Den

Why did the vampire bats hanging in the
church belfry look exactly the same
as each other ?

They were dead ringers !

Why didn't the spook win the lottery ?

He didn't have a ghost of a chance !

Why did the ghost of Guy Fawkes go crazy ?

It's OK, he just lost his head for a moment !

SOME MONSTER HOLIDAYS

Good Fryday !
(Good for frying anyone who gets close enough to grab !)

Eater Sunday and Eater Monday !
(Monsters don't have eggs !)

Guy Forks Night !
(Stay at home on November 5th if you're called Guy !)

Three girls were
exploring an old haunted house.
In one room they saw a £50 note on an old table.

The first girl went to pick it up when she heard
a ghostly voice saying,
"I'm the ghost of Auntie Mabel, that £50 stays
on the table !"

The second girl also tried to pick it up when the
voice called out
"I'm the ghost of Betty Grable, that £50 stays
on the table !"

The third girl marched straight into the room
and pocketed the £50. Before the ghost could
speak she called out,
"I'm the ghost of Davy Crockett, that £50 is
in my pocket !"

FOOLISH FOLLY

How do you make hot cross buns ?

Turn their central heating up too high !

Just because your hand is 12 inches long, that doesn't mean that it's a foot !

How do you confuse an idiot ?

I'll tell you tomorrow !

What does Tarzan eat on Saturday nights ?

Fish and chimps !

Did you hear about the idiot who went to a car boot sale ?

He now owns six car boots !

Did you hear about the man who joined the army because
he wanted to be a drill sargeant ?

They gave him a Black & Decker !

What happens when a witch catches the flu ?

Everyone gets a cold spell !

Did you hear where the stonemason took his girlfriend ?

To a rock concert !

Did you hear where the fizzy drinks maker
took his girlfriend ?

To a pop concert !

What does an idiot do when he wins the round the World
yacht race ?

He does a lap of honour !

What happened when the idiot made a paper plane ?

Someone hijacked it !

My dad says that in the future all trains and buses will run on time !

Rubbish, they'll still run on petrol like they do now !

Why did the idiot apply for a job as a language teacher ?

Because someone told him he spoke perfect rubbish !

Waiter, can I have my lunch on the patio ?

Certainly, Sir, but most people find a plate more sensible !

Why did the monster swallow a bag full of pennies?

Because he thought the change would do him good!

Why was the trout's piano off key?

Because he couldn't find the piano tuna!

I bought myself a pocket calculator for Christmas – now I know exactly how many pockets I have!

Why did the skeleton not go to the dance?

Because he had no body to go with!

Why should you never tell secrets in a corn field?

Because you would be surrounded by ears!

Did you hear about the failed magician?

He had one half brother and one half sister!

Mmmmm! This jam sponge cake is
lovely and warm!

**It should be, the cat's been sitting on
it all afternoon!**

Why did the robot need a manicure?

He had rusty nails!

What did the werewolf say to the vampire?

It's been so nice getting to gnaw you!

Why couldn't the butterfly go to the dance?

It was a moth ball!

Why couldn't the butterfly go to the dance?

What is the difference between Sting and Walt Disney?

Sting sings, but Walt Disney!

What deep sea creature swims about in his underwear?

The Loch Vest Monster!

Why were the naughty eggs sent out of the class?

For playing practical yolks!

Why did the bakers work late?

Beacuse they kneaded the dough!

When the monster had finished eating his human, he threw the wristwatch onto a pile in the corner.

His friend asked him why he did this.

"It's too time consuming," was his fellow monster's reply !

What do space monster sweet shops sell ?

Mars bars, Galaxy and Milky way !

What can you hold but never touch ?

Your breath !

Why did the man jump up and down after taking his medicine ?

Because he forgot to shake the bottle before he took it !

What are dog biscuits made from ?

Collie - flour !

What do you get if you cross a canary with a monster?

A broken cage!

What do you get if you cross a vampire with
a petrol pump?

**Something that makes a hole in your car and sucks out all
the petrol!**

Why are vampires so stupid?

Because blood is thicker than water!

Why can you never trick the snake monster ?

Because you can't pull his leg !

Did you hear about the idiot who sold his
television to raise the money to
buy a video ?

What do you get if you cross a bird with a snake ?

A feather boa constrictor !

Did you hear about the sculptor's son ?

He was a chip off the old block !

What's the difference between margarine and a goat ?

You mean you can't tell margarine from butter ?

Did you hear about the idiot who sold his
television to raise the money to
buy a video ?

**Or his brother, who sold his personal stereo,
to get the money to buy batteries for it !**

FOOLISH FOLLY

Did you hear about the triangle player who disappeared
from the orchestra.....

....while they were playing the Bermuda waltz ?

Did you hear about the librarian who got carried away....

....while he was reading
The Invasion Of The Body Snatchers ?

Waiter, waiter -there's a fly in my soup !

Sorry, madam, I didn't know you were vegetarian !

I'm never going to follow in my father's footsteps,
I faint at the sight of blood !

Was your father a doctor ?

No, a vampire !

What do you think the invention of the safety
match had on society ?

I'd say it was a striking achievement !

Why is a lazy schoolboy the exact opposite
of Robinson Crusoe ?

**Because Robinson Crusoe got all his work
done by Friday !**

You look depressed – I thought you had just started your
new job as a football boot cleaner ?

**I have – that's why I'm depressed –
I work for the centipede's eleven !**

Why should you always be thankful to pigs ?

**Because you should never take
them for grunted !**

Three badly made robots were playing cards...

One threw his hand in....

Another rolled his eyes – across the floor...

The third one laughed his head off !

A really bad jazz band had just finished a song.

"Any requests?" they called to the audience.

"Do you know "San Francisco ?", replied
one member of the audience.

"Yes, of course," replied the band leader.

"Please go there and play."

Two idiots were fishing in a lake, and were catching lots of fish.

They decided to come back the following weekend and catch even more fish, but they were concerned that they would not be able to find the exact spot on the lake when they next came.

Then one of them had a brilliant idea – he painted a red X on the side of the boat !

Why should you never fall asleep on a train ?

Because they run over sleepers !

What sort of chocolate bars do snowmen eat ?

Snowflakes !

YOU KNOW IT'S A BAD SIGN WHEN...

...you see weather men eating beans !

...travel agents close their shops and go on holiday !

...psychiatrists keep changing their minds !

...there's a fight in the chip shop, and
people get battered !

...people call in a sturgeon when they get a fish bone stuck
in their throat !

...a schoolboy gets locked in a cage in the classroom
because he is teacher's pet !

...a maths teacher smiles !

...the plumber brings a plug for your new bath, because he
thinks it is electric !

✎

What do you get if you cross a science
room and a dog ?

A Lab !

Do you play the Trumpet Voluntary?

No, my mum makes me do it!

How do you know when your school bus is old?

The seats are covered in Mammoth hide!

What do they say to postmen when they make them redundant?

"We are going to have to unsack you!"

What do you call a cake you eat in the bath?

Sponge!

Remember that before you give someone a piece of your mind, you should always check that you will have enough left over for yourself!

If I should win the lottery,

Think how much fun my life would be.

No more school, or work at home,

No more school dinners that taste like foam.

No more lines, no more pain,

Just lots of telly and sweets and games.

What do you call the place where all the used lottery tickets are thrown ?

The National Littery !

A man of 6 feet 9 inches and another man of 4 feet 6 inches robbed a bank today....

....police are looking high and low !

Why do swimming teachers like elephants ?

Because they always bring their trunks !

What do you call a man who can complete any
job in 30 seconds?

Arthur Minute!

What happened when two wasps had a fight?

There was a terrible BUZZZTUP!

Name seven things that are grey, four legged and have a
trunk!

Six elephants and a mouse going on holiday!

Why did the elephant cover his trunk in suncream?

Because he didn't want to get it sunburned!

How does a witch-bride get to the altar?

On a Groom Stick!

What sort of crisps do really nasty monsters eat ?

Squeeze and bunion !

Did you hear about the elephant who sued the airline ?

His trunk got caught in the X-ray machine !

Why do policemen like discos ?

They like a good steady beat !

What does a witch take on holiday ?

Her sleeping hag !

What was the Chinese air force commander called ?

The Wing commander !

Where does Dracula go in the summer ?

A holiday vamp !

Why is Cinderella so bad at football ?

She has a pumpkin for a coach !

Why do witches go to hot countries ?

For a spell in the sun !

FOOLISH FOLLY

Did you hear about the girl who put her granny's false teeth under her pillow ?

The tooth fairy left her a counterfeit £10 note !

What do you call the sea monster that dresses scruffily ?

Loch Vest !

Why did the farmworker punch the man in a pub ?

Because the man was eating the ploughman's lunch !

What did the doctor say to the invisible man after he had swallowed some coins ?

I can't see any change in you !

What insect do you find before the sea ?

The B !

Boy – Dad, am I worth £1000 to you ?

Dad – Of course you are son !

Boy – So, taking account of the 9 greenhouse windows I just smashed I reckon you owe me about £850 !

What do you dial if you want to contact the German police ?

Nein, Nein, Nein !

What do monsters eat with their Christmas dinner ?

Boy sprouts !

How do you cut water ?

With a sea-saw !

What does a Scottish owl do ?

Hoots, mon !

A man decided to start a chicken farm.. He bought 24 chicks to get started.

A week later he bought another 24 and then another 24 the week after that.

When his friend asked how his chicken farm was coming along the man replied...

"Not one of them has grown yet. I wonder if I'm planting them too deep ?"

What choice do you get with school custard ?

Like it or lump it !

How do you make a Swiss roll ?

Push him down an Alp !

What sweet course do solicitors like best ?

Sue - it pudding !

What do you get if you cross a vampire and an ice monster ?

Frost bite !

Teacher – I'll teach you to be clever in *my* class !

Pupil – At last - a lesson I'll be interested in!

Why did the deaf Italian waiter smear pasta sauce on people's ankles ?

Because he thought they asked for spagetti below the knees !

What do you get from a nudist pig?

Streaky bacon!

What did Fred Flintstone shout when he had a cold?

Yabba - Dabba - Atish - ooo!

What travels along the sea bed at 90 miles an hour?

Hondawater sea creatures!

What is the difference between electricity and lightning?

Lightning is free!

What sort of animal do you need when it's cold?

An otter!

Why do my schoolfriends call me a vampire?

**Don't let them worry you –
just drink your tea before it clots!**

A bird in the hand – is likely to poo on your wrist!

Where do space monks live?

In a Moon - astry!

Where do they keep old cows ?

In a MOOOseum !

Â·

What do you do if you swallow a wristwatch ?

Take a laxative to help pass the time !

Â·

Why did the lemon refuse to fight the orange ?

Because it was yellow !

Â·

What is always dressing ?

Mayonnaise !

Â·

Knock, Knock
Who's there ?
Howard.
Howard who ?
Howard I know ?

My friend John believes in free speech –

**which is why he comes round to my house
to telephone people !**

✑

What is a Forum ?

A two – um plus a two – um !

✑

The new doctor is so witty - he'll have you in stitches !

**I hope not - I've only come to see him
about my sore throat !**

✑

Catacomb - hair cleaning device for cats !

✑

A load of bees were getting very hot
and bothered one summer's day.
The queen bee asked what the trouble was...

"Swarm" came the reply !

What do you give a pig with a sore bottom ?

Oinkment !

✎

In the olden days, false teeth were made of wood –

– do you know what tree the wood came from ?

The Gum Tree ?

✎

What did the careful robot say ?

Look before you bleep !

✎

Teacher – Blenkinsop, what is a telescope ?

**Blenkinsop – something that you can watch TV with
from a long way off ?**

✎

Why are dinosaurs extinct ?

**Because male and female dinosaurs refused to get evolved
with each other !**

Why was the ghost's son asked to leave the school?

Because he was clearly too high spirited!

How many letters in hungry horse?

Four – M. T. G. G.!

Why was the genie in the lamp angry?

Someone rubbed him up the wrong way!

What is yellow and white and travels at
125 miles an hour?

A train driver's egg sandwich!

What do you get if you cross a space suit
and a saddle ?

A Horse - tranaut !

What is the best thing to do when a hippo sneezes ?

Get out of the way !

I'd like to buy a teapot please !

Have you tried Boots ?

Yes, but it comes out through the lace holes !

Our tyres are the best that money can buy –
we skid you not !

Why do football teams have to practise so much when they
play against zombies ?

Because they face stiff competition !

What do you get if you cross an athlete
and a computer ?

A floppy discus thrower !

What is red and cheeky ?

Tomato sauce !

Which age did the mummies live in ?

The band - age !

Why did you decide to become a cat burglar ?

My doctor told me to take things quietly !

Why do flamingoes lift one leg ?

Because if they lifted both legs they would fall over !

What was the first thing that Henry VIII
did on coming to the throne ?

He sat down !

How many sheep does it take to make a sweater ?

Wow – I didn't even know sheep could knit !

How do you make gold soup ?

Put 14 carrots in it !

Operator - get me the king of the jungle !

I'm sorry but the lion is busy right now !

Why did the idiot fall asleep in a bakery ?

He went there for a long loaf !

What happened when the monsters ate the comedian ?

It was a feast of fun !

Waiter - this lemonade is cloudy !

No it isn't, sir, it's the glass that's dirty !

Why did the burglar break into the music shop ?

He was after the lute !

FOOLISH FOLLY

My uncle spent £1000 having his family tree traced!

Crikey – I hope he didn't find out that I cut it down!

Blenkinsop, what are you doing standing out
there in the rain?

Getting wet!

What do you call a man with a speedometer on his head?

Miles!

Have you been drinking your medicine
after your bath ?

**No, after I have drunk the bath I just can't
manage the medicine !**

What do you call a pimple on a Tyrannosaurus Rex ?

A Dino-sore !

Our parrot lays star-shaped eggs !

Wow - does it talk as well ?

It just says the one word - OUCH !

Grandad, do you know how to
impersonate a frog ?

I think so, young Eric, but why ?

Because Mum says that when you
croak we'll be rich !

FOOLISH FOLLY

What kind of bow is never tied?

A Rainbow!

What did the clockmaker say when he was burgled?

He's taken my valuable time!

What's bright red, runs on petrol and eats cornflakes?

A motor cycle – I lied about the cornflakes!

What did the fat man say when he sat down at
the dinner table?

"Just think – all this food is going to waist!"

What sort of books do dwarves read?

Collections of short stories!

Why did the burglar buy a surf board?

He wanted to start a crime wave!

What did the bull say when he came back
from the china shop?

I had a really smashing time!

What's the special offer at the pet shop this week?

Buy one cat – get one flea!

When do 2 and 2 make more than 4?

When they make 22!

Why should you never listen too closely to the match?

Because you might burn your ears!

POTTY POEMS

Mary had a little lamb,
and a little pony, too.
She put the pony in a field,
and the lamb into a stew!

Humpty Dumpty sat on a wall,
Humpty Dumpty had a great fall.
All the king's horses and
all the king's men,
thought it was really funny,
and asked him to do it again!

A Yeti who came from Basmati,
Woke up one day feeling quite hearty.
It's those climbers I ate,
He said as he licked the plate.
I can't wait for the rescue party!

Simple Simon
met a pieman
going to the fair.
Said Simple Simon
to the pieman,
may I taste your wares ?
Said the pieman
to Simple Simon,
I don't sell wares
but you can try one of my pies if you like !

I wandered lonely as a cloud
that floats on high o'er hill and dell.
No-one would sit next to me
'cos I had made a nasty smell !

If you can pass exams,
while all about you are failing theirs,
you're a bigger swot than I am,
Gunga Din !

To be or not to be
that is the question,
or should I just use a pen instead!

Little Miss Muffet
sat on her tuffet
eating her favourite lunch.
A giant went by
looking up to the sky
and Little Miss Muffet went 'CRUNCH'.

Little Bo-Peep
has lost all her sheep,
which is why she's down at the
job centre this morning!

I went to the pictures tomorrow,
I got a front row seat at the back,
I bought an ice cream with a cherry on top,
I ate it and gave it them back !

The animals went in two by two,
the elephant and the kangaroo,
the lion the tiger,
the cat and the dog,
the mouse the gorilla,
the rat and the frog,
but they could only find one dinosaur,
which is why they aren't around any more !

Roses are red, violets are blue
You look like a codfish
And smell like one too !

249

Little Jack Horner,
sat in the corner,
eating his apple pie.
He put in his thumb,
and pulled out a plum,
and said 'that's a
funny looking apple!'

Hickory Dickory Dock,
6 mice ran up the clock.
The clock struck one,
but the other 5
got away!

Jack and Jill
went up the hill
to fetch a pail of water,
Jack fell down
and broke his crown
and Jill said
I told you you shouldn't
try and skateboard down...

A green spotted alien from Mars
liked eating motorcycles and cars.
When people cried 'shame'
he said 'It's the same...
as you lot eating Mars bars !'

We're going to build a bonfire,
put our maths books on the top,
put school dinners in the middle
and burn the bloomin lot !

Glory, glory alleyluyah
teacher hit me with a ruler
the ruler broke in two and
so she hit me with her shoe
and I wish I was at home...

At lunchtime every schoolday,
Blenkinsop (the fat),
would eat his way through everything,
except the kitchen cat.
Two plates of chips, for starters,
a pack of crisps (or three),
then on to shepherd's pie and beans,
washed down with mugs of tea.
Spaghetti Bolognese and rice,
it all went down a treat,
chicken curry, very nice,
pasties (cheese and meat).
When all the savouries had been
dispatched into his belly,
he started on the sweet menu,
(say goodbye to the jelly !)
rice pudding, jam and eccles cakes,
yogurt, custard, shortbread,
till suddenly he simply burst,
on the final slice of bread.

When Mary had a little lamb
the doctor was surprised,
but when Old Macdonald had a farm
he couldn't believe his eyes !

*School, glorious school,
we love all our teachers,
our lessons are cool,
but some pupils are creatures.*

Mary had a little lamb,
which she dressed in pretty blouses.
She also had a ferret,
which she put down her dad's trousers !..

WHAT IF ?

If I were a schoolboy,
All over again,
I'd work really hard,
And never get the cane.
I'd pass exams,
Just like that,
I'd even remember,
To wear my cap.
Then one day,
If my dream came true,
I'd be a teacher,
Just like you !
I hope you like my poem,
I don't want to make you sad, but....
It was written by a boy,
Who is totally MAD !

I once met a man from Hong Kong,
who'd been jogging for twenty years long.
He was terribly sweaty,
- he looked like a yeti,
and his feet had a terrible pong !

I love all my teachers,
from my head down to my belly.
I love to do my homework,
even though I miss the telly.
I love to do detention,
and I love to work real late.
I polish all the teachers shoes,
I really think they're great.
They're kind and smart and helpful,
they're delicate and gentle.
And I am - yes, you've guessed it -
very, very mental !

A rather dim gardener from Leeds,
once swallowed a packet of seeds.
In just a few weeks,
his ears turned to leeks,
and his hair was a tangle of weeds !

Mary had a little fox,
it ate her little goat,
now everywhere that MAry goes,
she wears her fox-skin coat !

I never could
quite work out why
an elephant
could never fly.
With massive ears
to flap and twitch
you'd think they'd glide
without a hitch.

Little Miss Muffet
sat on a tuffet,
eating tandoori and rice.
A monster from Bury
ate Miss Muffet and curry
and said by george that was nice !

WHO, WHAT, WHEN WHERE, WHY ?

What sort of music do you hear most in the jungle ?

Snake, rattle and roll !

Why are you taking that shovel to youir singing class ?

So I can get to the low notes !

Who runs the pub in the jungle ?.

The wine-ocerous !

Why did the cannibal go the wedding ?

Because he heard they were going to toast the bride and groom !

Why were you breaking the speed limit ?

I was trying to get home before my petrol ran out !

Why did the sprinter run across everyone
sitting in the park ?

Because his trainer told him to run over twenty laps !

Where were all the Kings and Queens of
France crowned ?

On the head !

What did the drama teacher say to you ?

**She said I've got the perfect
face for radio !**

Why was the baby goat a crazy mixed up kid ?

Because he fell into the spin dryer !

What makes you think my son could be an astronaut ?

...he has nothing but space between his ears !

What were all you children before you
started school ?

"Happy !"

When are you allowed to take toffee to school ?

On a chews day !

Why do doctors hate teachers when they
come to see them ?

**Because they never give them enough time
to do the examination !**

Why did the school idiot buy a sea horse ?

Because he wanted to play water polo !

How long is a school ome lette ?

Don't be daft - it's round just like any other sort !

Why did the green, slimy space monster go
to see Jurassic Park ?

Because he had read the book and really enjoyed it !

What did the farmer say when the townie
asked him if he had any hay ?

Stacks !

What sort of wallpaper do birds like best ?

Flock !

What do you do with a giant deck of playing cards ?

Big deal !

What is sheepskin useful for ?

Keeping the sheep's insides where they belong !

What is the best time to pick apples ?

When the farmer is away on holiday !

Why are teachers always welcome in snooker halls ?

Becasue they always bring their own chalk !

When God made a woman out of a man's rib –
what did he do with all the leftovers ?

When my sewing teacher returned to school after being ill I
asked how she was feeling and she said...

"Sew, sew !"

What did Snow White say as she looked through her empty
photograph album ?

"Some day my prints will come !"

Why did Belinda give cough medicine to the pony ?

Because Sally told her it was a little horse !

When the teacher asked the class to write an essay about what they would do if they won the lottery

Blenkinsop handed in a blank sheet of paper.

"What is the meaning of this?" she asked.

"It's what I'd do if I won the lottery – nothing!"

When Melissa was playing the flute

Her brother said, "you should be on the television playing that!"

"Wow, do you think I'm good enough?" she replied.

"No, but at least I could turn you off!"

Why do monsters have to pay twice when
they go to the zoo ?

Once to get in and once to get out !

Where do teachers get all their information ?

From fact-ories !

What did one salt pot maker say to the other
salt pot maker when they first met ?

Shake !

What did the alien say to the petrol pump ?

"Take your finger out of your ear when I'm talking to you !"

Why do monsters not mind being eaten
by kindly ghosts ?

**Because they know they will always
be in good spirits !**

Why did the crocodile buy his son a camera ?

Because he was always snapping !

Doctor, doctor, my sister thinks she's a lift !

You had better tell her to come in and see me !

I can't – she doesn't stop at this floor !

I met my first girlfriend at a printmaker's disco –

But it didn't last, she wasn't the right type for me !

What would you do if a jellyfish stung you ?

I'd break every bone in its body !

What did the schoolboy bite the dentist ?

Because he got on his nerves !

What do mice sing at birthday parties ?

For cheese a jolly good fellow !

How does Father Christmas begin a joke ?

This one will sleigh you... !

What does a toad use for making furniture ?

A toad's tool !

How do you make a cat happy?

Send it to the Canary Isles!

Why was the boy who had cake upset?

Because it was stomach cake!

How did the schoolgirl swim at over 60 mph?

She swam over a waterfall!

Why was Cinderalla rubbish at games ?

Because her coach was a pumpkin !

What were the 16 schoolboys playing in the
telephone box ?

Squash !

What were Tarzan's last words ?

Who moved that vine !

What work does Mrs Claus give Santa Claus to do
in the garden ?

Ho Ho Hoeing !

What did they call the cowboy after
someone stole all his cash ?

Skint Eastwood !

How did the schoolboy stop the elephant from smelling ?

He tied a knot in its trunk !

How should you show your appreciation to a vampire ?

With a fang-you letter !

Blenkinsop - you are good at picking up music -
go and move the piano from the music room
to the assembly hall !

Why does this homework look as though it has been written by your father ?

Well it would do, I borrowed his pen !

How does a woman know when she has fallen in love with a
cricket player ?

She is completely bowled over !

How do you help Frankenstein's monster ?

Give him a hand when he needs it !

What does it mean when the barometer falls ?

It means my dad is useless at knocking nails into the wall !

What can you tell me about the Dead Sea ?

I didn't even know it was sick !

What happened to the Scottish schoolboy who washed his kilt ?

Now he can't do a fling with it !

What do you call a prisoner's budgie ?

A jail bird !

Where would you find a 10,000 year old cow ?

In a Moooseum !

How do you wake chickens in the morning ?

With an alarm cluck !

What is a maybe ?

A bee born in May !

Why are mummies good at writing exams ?

Because they keep everything under wraps !

How do you keep a fool waiting...?

I'll tell you tomorrow !

What has 22 legs and 2 wings but can't fly ?

The school football team !

What is the name of that teacher with soil on his head ?

Pete !

Which famous knight never won a single battle ?

Sir Endor !

What do you call a man with a tree growing
out of his head ?

Ed - Wood !

How do you stop a head cold going to your chest ?

Easy - tie a knot in your neck !

Why shouldn't you try to swim on a full stomach ?

Because it's easier to swim on a full swimming pool !

What creature sticks to the bottom of sheep ships ?

Baaa - nacles !

How do you know if your little brother is turning
into a fridge ?

**See if a little light comes on whenever he opens
his mouth !**

What is the coldest part of the North Pole ?

An explorer's nose !

What do computer operators
eat for lunch ?

Chips !

Why is that man standing in the sink?

He's a tap dancer!

Where do rabbits learn to fly?

In the Hare Force!

How did the witch know she was getting better?

**Because the doctor let her get
out of bed for a spell!**

What did the witch call her baby daughter ?

Wanda !

How do witch children listen to stories ?

Spellbound !

Which witch went to Ipswich ?
The rich witch called little Mitch,
with the light switch for the soccer pitch,
who twitched and fell in a ditch;
that witch went to Ipswich –
and never came home !

What would you find in a rabbit's library?

Bucks!

Where do fish like going for their holidays?

Finland!

What did the overweight ballet dancer perform?

The dance of the sugar plump fairy!

Why is it easy to swindle a sheep ?

Because it is so easy to pull the wool over its eyes !

What do elves eat at parties ?

Fairy Cakes !

What do you get if you cross a brain surgeon
and a herd of cows ?

Cow-operation !

Why did the carpenter go to the doctor ?

He had a saw hand !

Why did the doctor operate on the man who
swallowed a pink biro ?

He had a cute-pen-inside-is !

Why are you
putting Mr Smith's left
leg in plaster, it's his
right leg that's broken ?

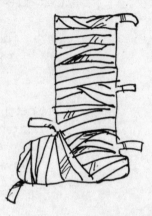

It's OK, I'm new so I'm
practising on the left
one first to make sure
I do it properly!

What sort of fish would
you find in a bird cage ?

A Perch !

What sort of fish would
you find in a shoe ?

An Eel !

What do you call a cowboy who helps out in a school ?

The Deputy Head !

What do you call the teacher in the school who gives out forms that you have to fill in ?

The Form Teacher !

Did you hear about the dog who was arrested ?

He didn't pay a barking ticket !

Where did the rich cat live?

In a mews cottage!

What position did the witch play in the football team?

Sweeper!

What position did the pile of wood play in the football team?

De-fence!

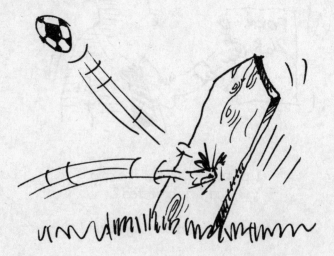

Why couldn't the slow boxer get a drink at the party ?

Because everyone beat him to the punch !

Why was the archaeologist upset ?

His job was in ruins !

Why was the butcher worried ?

His job was at steak !

Why did the teacher have to turn the lights on ?

Because his pupils were so dim !

Why did the French farmer only keep the one chicken ?

Because in France one egg is un oeuf !

What did the farmer say when all his cows
charged him at once ?

I'm on the horns of a dilemma here !

What sort of snake will tell on you ?

A grass snake !

Why did the doll blush ?

Because she saw the Teddy Bear !

What do you get if you cross a frog and a fizzy drink ?

Croaka - cola !

What do you call a German barber ?

Herr Dresser !

Why do teddy bears never hear what you say ?

Because they have cloth ears !

Who serves the food on a spooky aeroplane ?

The Air Ghostess !

What sort of ring is always square ?

A boxing ring !

What sort of queue is always straight ?

A snooker one !

What sort of net is useless for catching fish ?

A football net !

Why do people leave letters at the football ground ?

They want to catch the last goal-post !

I've got a terrible fat belly !

Have you tried to diet ?

Yes, but whatever colour I use it still looks fat !

What do you call a
frog that helps
children safely
across the street ?

The green cross toad !

Did you hear about
the posh chef
with an attitude
problem ?

**He had a french
fried potato on
his shoulder !**

Why do golfers carry a spare sock?

Because they might get a hole in one!

Did you hear about the man who went to the doctor and told him he thought he was a piano?

The doctor gave him a note!

What do you get if you cross a pig with a hedgehog?

A porkupine!

What do you call a wobbly book full of telephone numbers?

A jellyphone directory!

What sort of fish flies a spaceship?

A Pilot Whale!

What book do you buy to teach children
how to fight ?

A scrapbook !

What sort of animals make the best TV presenters ?

Gnus - readers !

What sort of animal is best at getting up
in the morning ?

A LLama clock !

How did you invent gunpowder?

I was using some candles to light my laboratory and it came to me in a flash!

How is your other invention coming along – you know, the matches?

Oh! They've been a striking success!

Why did the doctor take his nose to pieces?

He wanted to see what made it run!

Why is it dangerous to tell jokes to Humpty Dumpty?

He might crack up!

Blenkinsop - stop acting the fool -
I'm in charge of this class, not you !

Why do pens get sent to prison ?

To do long sentences !

What does a mouse say when you take his photo ?

Cheese !

What is the name of the detective who sings
quietly to himself while solving crimes ?

Sherlock Hums !

Why did the farmer feed his pigs sugar and vinegar ?

He wanted sweet and sour pork !

What do you call
the Scottish
dentist ?

Phil McCavity !

Why is the soil
in my garden
always dry ?

**Because you
have leeks !**

What kind of rose
has a bark ?

A dog rose !

What did the little
boy say when he
wanted his big
brother to give him
back his building
bricks ?

Lego !

Why are you called
Postman Pat ?

**Because I have to
deliver post to all
the farms !**

Which two words in the English
language have the most letters
?

Post Office !

How do you start a jelly baby race?

Ready - Set - Go!

What sort of music was invented by fish?

Sole music!

What gets smaller the more you put in it?

A hole in the ground!

Why is there a dead fly in my soup ?

**Waiter – Well, you surely don't expect to get
a live one at these prices !**

What happened to the man who
stole a lorry load of eggs ?

He gave himself up – he said he only did it for a yolk !

Did you know this is a one-way street !

I'm only going one way !

Yes, but everyone else is going the other way !

Well, you're a policeman, make them turn round !

What is the thing that is most read at Christmas ?

Rudolph's nose !

How do penguins get to school?

On 21 speed mountain icicles!

Why do cows have horns?

Because they would look pretty silly
with bells on their heads!

What do you get if you cross a fruit and a woman
who needs help?

A damson in distress!

What do you get if you train a reindeer to
be a hairdresser?

Styling Mousse!

What is a vampire's favourite sport?

Point to point!

What goes MOOOOOZ ?

A jet flying backwards !

What do blacksmiths eat for breakfast ?

Vice Crispies !

Why do toolmakers always escape from fires ?

They know the drill !

What self defence method do mice use ?

Ka - rat - e !

What did the stupid burglar do when he saw
a 'WANTED' poster outside the police station?

He went in and applied for the job!

What is a big game hunter?

Someone who can't find the football stadium!

Why are you putting that apple in the rowing boat?

You told me to put the cox in!

When 30 people were sheltering under an umbrella,
how many of them got wet ?

None - it wasn't raining !

Why are burglars such good tennis players ?

**Because they spend such a lot of their time
in courts !**

What do monsters fasten their suitcases to
the car roof-rack with ?

Frankentwine !

Is that a new perfume I smell?

It is, and you do!

What do vampires use to phone relatives?

A terror - phone!

What are wasps favourite flowers?

Bee - gonias!

Why did the fly fly ?

Because the spider spied her !

What sort of monster is musical ?

The one with A Flat head !

Where do Chinese vampires live ?

Fang - Hai !

What goes moo, moo, splash ?

A cow falling into the sea !

301

Why did the Romans build straight roads ?

They didn't want anyone hiding round the corners !

What do you call a dinosaur that
keeps you awake at night ?

Bronto - snore - us !

What is the name of the Australian dog drummer ?

Dingo Starr !

ALPHABET ANTICS

A

Artichoke   – a joke that artists tell each other !

Abacus   – swear word used by an aba !

Address Book – large book where women keep their clothes !

Aeroplane   – tool used to make wooden flying machines !

Agent   – someone who is polite !

Alarm clock – timepiece that scares everybody !

Algebra   – underwear worn by female alge !

Ambush   – place where pigs like to sleep !

Appetite   – when you can't eat because your belt is too tight!

Astronaut   – nothing in space!

B

Baby   - small bee !

Batchelor   - unmarried vampire !

Bacon   - what you eat on fry day !

Ballet   - form of entertainment that is tu tu wonderful !

Bank   - side of river where voles keep their money !

Barbecue   - line of people waiting to buy toy dolls !

Bark   - the sound a tree makes !

Bat   - what vampires use to play cricket with !

Battery   - what the school cook was
arrested for !

Bed   - where the idiot planted his
light bulbs !

Bell   - the kids round here will steal anything
- now the school bell's gone !

Bewitched   - a bee that has upset a witch !

Bookworm   - something that is always having
to eat its words !

Boomerang – a bent stick that is impossible to throw away!

Boxer – dog that starts punching when it hears a bell ring!

Bricklayer – chicken fed on sand and cement!

Broomstick – something that makes witches fly off the handle!

Buffalo – similar to a bison, but you can't wash your hands in a buffalo!

Bulldog – like a sheepdog – but for cows!

Butter – another name for goat!

C

Cabbage   – how old a taxi is !

Camel   – plural = camelot !

Canary   – bird that comes in a tin !

Cannibal   – someone who is always pleased
       to eat you !

Captain   – cap that comes in a tin !

Cartoon   – a song you sing in the car !

Catapult – weapon used by cats !

Caterpillar – column used to hold up a cat's home !

Cheesecake – served at a mouse's birthday party !

Chicken – something that always speaks
with fowl language !

Chirrup of figs – what you give to a
constipated budgie !

Circus – knight of old who invented the
big top !

Cliff – man with seagulls on his head !

Coconut – someone who loves cocoa !

Coffin   - what Dracula does a lot of
                when he has a cold !

Comb   - what bees do their hair with !

Comedian   - chicken that tells jokes !

Cowgirl   - female cow !

Crocodile   - telephone operator for alligators !

Cucumber   - curved snooker cue !

D

Dance   – something hens do chick to chick !

Dentist   – the first thing a vampire bites
after having a filling !

Desert   – pudding made from sand !

Dinner   – Batman's theme tune
(Dinner, Dinner, Dinner, Dinner, Batman !)

Dinosaur   – pimple on a T. Rex !

Dogfish   – cod with a personality problem !

Dogma   – mother of puppies !

Dollar Bill   – American !

Door catch - splinter that rips clothes
when you go into house !

Double glazing - two pairs of glasses !

Draculard - overweight vampire !

Drunk - empty glass !

Dynamite - then again she might not !

E

Ear — the opposite of there !

Eel — downtrodden fish !

Egypt — place where daddies are mummies !

Electrician — someone who does tricks with light bulbs !

Escalator — a moving stairway that makes you late for school !

Eskimo — escalator in a cold place !

F

Face pack   - box that ugly people keep their make up in!

Fairy ring   - goblin's telephone system!

False teeth - teeth that tell lies!

Fang mail   - what a vampire gets through the post!

Fatima   - overweight mother!

Feet   - what your shoes are when they measure 12 inches!

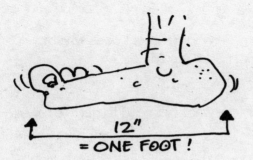

12" = ONE FOOT!

Female   - women posties !

Fencing team - people who put up fences !

Fiend   - almost a friend !

Filing cabinet - where cannibals keep all the spare fingernails !

Fish and ships - what a sea monster eats !

Flat mate   - what you get if you invite a giant monster round for tea !

Floodlight   - what Noah had on the ark to see where he was going !

Flu   - what an insect does when it has a cold !

Fly paper   - what flies read to get the news !

Foghorn — what cows use to find each other in the mist !

Fork Lift Truck - lorry used to pick up a giant's cutlery !

Fortune cookie - expensive biscuit !

Fountain pen - pen that runs on water !

Frankenstein – a self made man !

a man who made his own entertainment !

a man who kept people in stitches !

Frogspawn – a toad's chess piece !

Fur – a type of woolly tree !

Furniture – vege – tables are the sort of furniture that monsters eat !

G

Gamble — what naughty little lambs do !

Gangster — when criminals get together to bake a cake !

Garlic — something to make a vampire cross !

Geography — what you have to pay a geogra to get it to work for you !

Ghost train — what spooks travel on when they go on ghouliday !

Ghould — what spooks score in football !

Giant snails - what you find on the end of giant's fingers !

Gruesome - the wrong way to say that your daughter has grown !

Glass eyes - something that might just come out in conversation !

Gnome - a gnouse where elves live !

Goldfish - a fish that ate 24 carrots !

Gorilla - what a chimp puts bread under to make toast !

Granny flat - what you get if you invite a monster round for tea !

Graveyard - grave for a dwarf !

Greece   - what the school cook uses !

Greenhouse - home for aliens !

Guillotine   - guaranteed cure for dandruff !

H

Hairdresser - cupboard where a bald man keeps his wigs !

Hamlet - pig playing Shakespeare !

Hammock - bed for pigs !

Handicap - neat place to keep your hat !

Haunting - the sort of melodies that ghosts sing to each other !

Headgear - frankenstein's bolts !

Hellfire - get the sack from Satan !

Hindu — a party where you invite all your hin laws !

Hippie — one of the joints in your leggie !

Hole in one — why golfers carry a spare pair of trousers - in case they get a hole in one !

Honeycomb — what bees do their hair with !

Horse — when a pony has a sore throat !

Human beings — what cannibals like to eat on toast !

House — what you shout when you win a cottage at bingo !

I

Ice cream   – and so would you if you had just seen a ghost !

Ig   – eskimo house without a loo !

Icicle   – bicycle with a wheel missing !

Illness   – what the Loch Ness monster sometimes catches !

Ink   – what you get from a sheep when it's turned into a pen !

Inkling – a baby pen!

Invisible man – someone who has transparents!

Iron tablets – pills that do the laundry!

Italian wine – the sound that ghosts from Milan make!

J

Jack   - what you call a man with a car on his head !

Jack Frost - a man with an ice cream van on his head !

Jellyfish   - what monsters eat at parties !

Juggler   - the vein that Dracula visits the circus to see !

Jumper   - a cross between a sheep and a kangaroo !

Jungle sale   - where Tarzan buys his clothes !

K

Ketchup — what one sauce bottle shouts to another in a race !

Kick — what some people get out of doing karate !

Konga — a dance for big monkeys !

Kippers — sleeping fish !

Kitten — when a cat tells you a joke !

Knight — what you get if you knit with steel wool !

L

Ladder — the place where very tall people store their food!

Ladybird — female bird!

Lamb chops — what you get from a sheep who knows karate!

Landing — where jumbo jets will end up if you leave the lights on!

Lap   – what motor racing cats do a lot of !

Larder   – where the school cook keeps all her lard !

Legs   – what cannibals love to eat
– especially fried legs and bacon !

Lemonade – hearing aid for a lemon !

Lice   – what Australians tie up their shoes with !

Lid   – what Australians have in their pencils !

Liar   – dishonest lute !

Lighthouse – what a snail carries on its back !

Lion — if the lion is engaged you can't make any telephone calls in the jungle !

Lisp — Hith ith the thound a thnake with a lithp makesth !

Lizard — the magician in a snake's circus !

Loaf — what idle bread does !

Lonely heart – missing vampire's parcel !

Lone Ranger – the man who gets you a mortgage !

M

Mad — what happens when a vampire goes batty!

Maggot — a grub's favourite TV detective!

Mailman — opposite of female woman!

Manure — recyclable unmentionables!

Marriage lines — where you tie your wife or husband when a train is coming!

Meatball — what sausages play hockey with!

Meeting of minds — when two monsters run head first into each other!

Memory lapse - when you can't remember how
many times you've run round
the track!

Mercy - what vampires shout when they are
forced to eat garlicky French food!

Mermaid - a fish that mumbles!

Mexican - a can full of mexies!

Mice - how posh people say mouse!

Mole - a furry miner!

Money boxes - underpants that people keep
their cash in!

Monkey - what an ape opens his door with!

Moose   – pudding made from deer !

Moth ball   – dance where butterflies are
made welcome !

Mountaineer – what a mountain listens with !

Mummies   – daddies with an interest in
wrap music !

Mushroom   – when your dustbin is full of
toadstools, there's not
mushroom inside !

N

Nailbiter   - monster with a mouth full of metal !

Narrow squeak - the noise you hear when you
                          tread on a thin mouse !

Neck   - what vampires in love like to do best !

Necktie   - Frankenstein's bolt !

Nervous wreck - a sunken ship with a twitch !

Newspaper – what gnus read!

Night school – where vampires go to learn to read in the dark!

Nit nurse – someone who makes you a nice woolly hat to keep your nits warm!

Noah's ark – the first boat ever fitted with floodlights!

Note paper – for writing down music!

Nun – someone who can hide on a zebra crossing!

O

Octopus — cat with 8 legs!

Oil — there are two types.

Crude Oil — which floats on the sea and shouts "knickers!"

Refined Oil — which floats on the sea and says, quietly, "underpants!"

Oinkment — what you give a pig with pimples!

Onion — from the old saying —
"An apple a day keeps the doctor away, an onion a day keeps everyone else away!"

Orangeade — What you give a deaf fruit!

"PARDON?!"

Orchestra — an anagram of CARTHORSE — true!

p

Paddle   – how posh people say puddle !

Pane   – what you feel when you walk into a sheet of glass !

Parrot   – what the Chinese man called the man who flew the plane !

Peach   – what you can call anyone with a heart of stone !

Peanuts   – the sort of nuts you find in a pod !

Pear   – what the French apple called his dad !

Peas   – this is what we get at Christmas
– peas on earth and goodwill to all men !

Pedestrian   - why did the optician build his
shop in the new precinct ?
Because it had been
pedestrian - eyes - ed !

Pelican   - the sort of tin that pelis are
stored in !

Pen   - where a farmer keeps his sheep
and his ink !

Penguins   - something that polar bears never eat
- because they can't get the
wrappers off !

Phantom   – the sort of pen a ghost writes with
                      – a phantom pen !

Phoney   – someone who pretends he has a
                        telephone in his pocket !

Piano   – something you drop down a
                        mineshaft to get A Flat Minor !

Piece of pie – what's left after the cook has
                        dropped it on the kitchen floor !

Piglet   – a small house rented out to pigs !

Pigeon Toes – what you get if you put birdseed
                        in your shoes !

Plumber   – drain surgeon !

Poetry in motion – when the teacher throws an
                        English book across the room !

Poison Ivy   - the girl who has an effect on just
               about everybody !

Pole   - stick of wood found in the snow !

Policeman   - the man who lives at 999,
               Letsby Avenue !

Porcupine   - what you get if you cross a
               pig and a tropical fruit !

Pork chop   - what a pig that knows karate does !

Pottery in motion - when someone throws a
                      plate at you !

Prince   - what royalty have to give to the
               police if they are suspected of a
               crime - finger prince !

Printer   - a job you can only get if you
               happen to be the right type !

Promise — something that you have to give
to other people and keep as well !

Puffin — breathless bird !

Punch clock — how a boxer logs into work
each day !

Q

Quack — a duck doctor!

Queen bee — the one with a tiny crown!

Queue jumper — a sweater you give to a cold queue!

Quicksand — builder's material that runs away when you're not looking!

R

Rabbit — when a rabbit gets trapped under a sunbed, is he a hot cross bun?

Racing pigeon — the one with the crash helmet and the stripes down the wings!

Railway lines — what teachers give naughty railways to do!

Raining cats and dogs — when this happens be careful not to step in a poodle!

Red Indian — a tribe with all the know how they need!

Reincarnation — being born again as a can of evaporated milk!

Religious education exams - these are marked with a spirit level !

Reptile - special flat frogs that stick to bathroom walls !

Restaurant - a cruel place where they beat eggs, batter fish and whip cream !

Revolution - what the wheel caused when it was first invented !

Road hog - pig who drives badly !

Robin Banks - a man who steals for a living !

Robinson Crusoe - a man who took weekends off
                      - because he had all his work
                       done by Friday!

Robot - a thing with nerves of steel!

Rock concert - where you would go to hear
                The Rolling Stones!

Roller skates - dangerous wheeled fish!

Rome - a city that must have been built at
night - because we know it
wasn't built in a day!

Rose petal - what you have on a rose bicycle!

Row boat - a boat that sits patiently in line!

Rubbish collection - a job that you just pick up
as you go along !

Run over   - this will make you feel tyred !

Russia   - Knock, knock !
Who's there ?
Russia !
Russia who ?
Russia way - a monster's coming !

S

Sandwitch – a witch eating her packed lunch on the beach !

Santa claus – The creature who takes presents to monsters !

Saucer – where rivers start
– like the saucer the Nile for example !

Sausage roll – goes with sausage rock to make music !

School dinners – our daily dread !

Scratch card – what you use if you get fleas !

Second hand – what a used wristwatch has !

Secret — something that everyone except you knows!

Shadow boxing — putting shadows into containers!

Sheep dip — what sheep have at parties!

Sherlock Bones — the famous skeleton detective!

Shoe — what you shout to a gang of runaway trainers!

Shorts — half hearted trousers !

Shy — what coconuts are on their first date !

Sick jokes — what people in hospital tell each other !

Sign — seen outside the shipyard
— Gone To Launch !

Singing insects — humbugs !

Skateboard — fish used as transport by sharks !

Skeleton staff — people working in a graveyard !

Sledgehammer - what you take to school when you break up !

Sleeping pills - tablets that snore in the bottle !

Sleepers - people who fall asleep on railway tracks !

Slippers - shoes made from banana skins !

Slugs - very squishy, slimy bullets !

Smoker's cough - that's true !

Snails   - it's what you find at the end of your fingers !

Soap Opera - what you get if you sing in the bath or shower !

Soldiers   - heavily armed sticks of bread that go into action as soon as they see a shell !

Soup   - something that turns to gold if you put 14 carrots in it !

Space   - what you need between your ears if you want to be an astronaut when you leave school !

Spellbinding - the covers of a witches book !

Spelling — what witches have to learn at school!

Spirit level — what ghosts use to check that their walls are level!

Spook — when a ghost has already spooken!

Squash — the game elephants like to play
— by getting 3 of their friends in a phone box!

Statue   - what an idiot calls a telephone !

Stones   - the name of a rock band !

Stork   - creep up behind a bird with long legs !

String   - the sound you hear if your telephone is made from rope !

Styscraper - a multi storey home for pigs !

Sultan   - rich oil owning currant !

T

Tables — furniture you can eat - vegetables !

Tailor's Dummy - what a suit maker sucks when he's scared !

Tap dancer - someone who dances in the sink !

Tapeworms – what insects use to measure things !

Tarzan – someone who creeps up on you in the jungle !

Tea cosy – used to keep tea bags feeling comfy !

Teacher's pet – the child kept in the cage by the door !

Teenager – say red backwards
– now you are one !

Theatre – where ghosts go to see a phantomime at Christmas !

Thunder – what outdoor orchestras with good conductors should avoid !

Time – a herb with a wristwatch !

Tinder   - the Australian for tender !

Toadstools - what toads use for DIY !

Tomorrow - is not a very strong day
- in fact it's a weekday !

Tooth Fairy - the little fairy who will take out all
your teeth if you sleep with your
head under the pillow !

Toothbrush - what a tooth does its hair with
before it goes out !

Tortoise   - what our last teacher did !

Trains   - things that stop at devil crossings
when they travel through
monster country !

Trampolining - a sport that's up and down !

Travel Agent - someone that spies go to to
book a holiday !

Tree surgeons - 3 people operating on a person at
the same time !

Trifle deaf - what you are if you wake up with
jelly and cream in your ear !

U

Udder — when you tell a cow a tall story, she'll tell you to pull the udder one!

Umpire — the man who couldn't spell who designed the State Building in America!

Undertakers — people who have a great graveside manner!

Underpants — knickers worn in submarines!

V

Vampire — someone who is a little batty !

Varnish — disappear with a shiny finish !

Vast — the sort of bottom you see on a ship — 'A Vast Behind !'

Vegetable — where vegetarians eat their meals !

Venetian Blind — someone who has forgotten their glasses !

Vet, Vet, Vet — German band !

Vikings — ancient warriors who invented Norse Code !

Vinegar   – what a cat will drink to become
a sourpuss !

Violins   – used in robberies, robberies
with violins !

Viper   – snake used to clean car windscreen !

Vitamin B   – Bee who runs the health food shop !

W

Waiter — the first thing a monster eats in a restaurant !

Waspital — where you take sickly bees !

Watchdog — dog that goes, woof, woof, tick, woof, woof, tick !

Water — someone who cures warts !

Water polo — sport that you need a sea horse for !

Werewolves — that shoud read "we are wolves !"

Whale weigh station — where a whale gets weighed !

Whistle — what bees can't do, which is
why they buzz!

Witch doctor — where witches go when they're
not well!

Woodworm — something that says "it was nice
gnawing you," to your furniture!

X, Y, Z

X-Ray — ray after he gets hit by a bus!

Xylophone — what xylos telephone their mums and dads with!

Yak — talkative animal!

Yankee Doodle — American drawing!

Zombie — undead bee!

Zoo — what animal lawyers do!

SICKLY SMILES

WAITER, WAITER......

Hop into the kitchen and get me some frogs legs !

Fetch me a crocodile sandwich, and make it snappy !

Get me the 24 hour special, and don't be all day
about it !

Get me a bacon sandwich – for my porked lunch !

How do you keep flies out of your kitchen ?

Move the pile of rotting vegetables
into the lounge !

Which vegetable can count the highest ?

A pot 80 !

Who is that at the door ?

A man with a wooden leg called Smith !

Really – and what is his other leg called ?

Who is that at the door?

A man with no legs!

Sounds like a low down bum to me!

✏️

What does the cannibal plastic surgeon charge?

An arm and a leg!

✏️

Waiter – why is this dead mouse in my soup?

Terribly sorry, sir, it should be in the pudding!

A man was staying in a spooky hotel, when he
was woken in the middle of the night by an eerie
voice saying, "when I get you, I'm going to eat you!"

He ran down to the reception desk and demanded
an explanation from the manager. The manager went
up to the room with him and pulled open the
wardrobe door.

Inside was a monster, desperately trying to reach
a chocolate bar that he had dropped down the back.
He was muttering to himself, "when I get you,
I'm going to eat you!"

What do you call exams that have all the answers
pencilled in for you?

Easy S Es!

What do they call the competition when they draw
numbered balls out of a lavatory pan?

The National Pottery!

How do bees qualify to make honey?

They have to pass their hiving test!

What are white, scary and enable you to open any door?

Skeleton keys!

What do they call the competition when they draw numbered balls out of an old coffin?

The National Rottery!

What sort of people make the best ghosts?

The ones who are faint hearted!

Did you hear about the monster who carried on the family traditions...

...he was swallowing in his father's footsteps !

What does a vampire say if he is uncertain about something ?

"I'll suck it and see !

"What do you call a baby budgie ?

A Budget !

Why do chickens listen to the radio ?

It's their only form of hentertainment !

What sort of teeth can sing in a high voice ?

Falsetto teeth !

Why did the man send his alphabet soup back ?

Because he couldn't find words to describe it !

What sort of music can you listen to in bed ?

Sheet music !

How do fleas train ?

They have to start from scratch !

Football manager - why didn't you stop the ball ?

**Goalkeeper - I thought that's what these nets
were here for !**

These pavements are really greasy!

That's no surprise – the rain has been dripping all day!

What do you call pigs who write to each other?

Pen friends!

Excuse me, how long will the next taxi be?

About 2.3 metres!

What did the dog say when his owner stopped
him chewing the newspaper?

You took the words out of my mouth!

Blenkinsop – what is the definition of dieting?

Mind over fatter!

What is the only thing that you can lose, and yet still have ?

Your temper !

What has 50 feet but can't walk ?

A tape measure !

What has 100 feet but can't walk, and it's not a tape measure ?

A dead centipede !

What do old fish wear ?

Shawls !

Did you hear about the M.P. who was arrested ?

He tried to take his seat in the House of Commons, but he was seen by the security cameras !

Which profession gets most fringe benefits ?

Hairdressers !

In which job do you get the most perks ?

In a coffee shop !

What runs all day but is never short of breath ?

A train !

When can't you open a locked piano lid ?

When the keys are on the inside !

There is only one thing higher than a king - his crown !

What sort of eggs go into uncharted areas of the world ?

Egg - splorers !

What is a volcano ?

A headless mountain !

Why don't elephants believe in fairy stories ?

They don't hold with mumbo - jumbo !

What is the difference between a blue elephant
and an apple ?

Apples aren't blue !

Why do elephants have big ears ?

Because Noddy didn't pay the ransom !

What is huge, grey and has 12 feet ?

3 elephants !

What driver has never passed a test ?

A screwdriver !

What is the biggest mouse ever discovered ?

The hippopotamouse !

Why did the idiot drive his car off the side of a mountain ?

Because someone told him that it was fitted with air brakes !

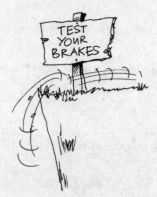

Why was the man laughing, even though his career
was in ruins ?

He was an archaeologist !

What did the clean dog say to the dirty dog ?

Long time no flea !

What do you give a monster with big feet ?

Big shoes !

What sort of holidays do cannibals never go on ?

Self catering !

What do you get if you cross a giant monster
with a frog ?

Something that can catch aeroplanes with
its tongue !

What do you call a rabbit's pram?

A buns buggy!

How do worms drive birds crazy?

By sleeping late - and never being the early bird!

What does a frog do when it dies?

It croaks!

When frogs see a rainbow they always look for the croak of gold at the end of it!

What sort of shoes do frogs wear in Summer?

Open toad sandals!

Why was the mother flea depressed ?

All her children had gone to the dogs !

✎

Why should you never go to the laundrette late
at night ?

**Because you have to remove your clothes
10 minutes before closing time !**

✎

Two children were paddling in the sea...

My, your feet are really dirty !

Well, we didn't come on holiday last year so what
do you expect !

✎

Why did the cannibals have indigestion ?

**He must have eaten someone who disagreed
with him !**

What did one sardine say to the other sardine
when he saw a submarine full of people ?

"You'll never get me into one of those things !"

Did you hear about the guard dog that loved raw onions
and garlic ?

His bark was much, much worse than his bite !

What does a vegetarian cannibal eat ?

Swedes !

Did you hear about the cowboy who only wore
one spur ?

He wanted his horse to run round in circles !

This garden is very light !

Yes, that's because I planted a lot of bulbs last year !

Why do ghosts go to the spring sales in the shops?

They enjoy bargain haunting!

A woman went into a petshop and asked if she could have a hamster for her son.

"Sorry," replied the shop keeper, "we don't do part exchange!"

My friend is so stupid that he thinks twice before saying nothing!

Let me tell you the joke about the mind reader....

....what do you mean you've already heard it!

What pets do monsters keep in glass bowls?

Ghoulfish!

I went to the ghostly circus last night
– to see the fright rope walker!

At what time should you avoid ghostly dogs and cats?

On the stroke of midnight!

Why are fish monsters musical?

They have their own set of scales!

Did you hear about the man who ran away with a
deer to get married?

They anteloped!

How do chickens tell their children off ?

They say 'cock-a-doodle-don't do that !'

Is it true that rabbits get their glasses
at the hoptician ?

Why did God give Moses some tablets ?

Moses said he had a headache !

What do dogs and trees have in common ?

Bark !

What do plumbers like to do in the garden ?

Plant leeks !

How does a witch tell the time ?

With a witch-watch !

A man was eating fish and chips when a little dog came along and started biting his trouser leg. He looked at the owner of the dog, who was doing nothing about this, and asked if it was all right to throw it a bit.

"Of course you can throw it a bit !" replied the owner.

The man picked up the dog and threw it over a fence into a pond !

How do you hire a car ?

Take the wheels off and stand it on some bricks !

The bionic android told his doctor that he thought he was going mad !

The doctor examined him, and agreed. "You've got a screw loose all right !"

Why did Arnie take a grenade launcher to a
birthday party ?

**Because someone told him he would have to blow
up the balloons !**

A man rescued a vampire from drowning, and the
vampire bit him as soon as they got onto dry land.
What did the man say ?

**"If that's all the fangs I get. I'll let you drown
next time !"**

How did the featherweight boxer do in his last fight ?

He tickled his opponent till he gave in !

Can you carry on playing football during a flood ?

Yes, you just have to bring on your subs !

What does a skeleton eat at a fast food restaurant ?

Ribs !

What is a prickly pear ?

Two hedgehogs !

What do you call a man with a map and a pair
of binoculars on his head ?

Seymour Miles !

What do you call an elephant wearing rubber boots ?

A wellyphant !

SICKLY SMILES

Caroline just got the sack. She worked for 8 hours a day,
and she slept for 8 hours a day.

Unfortunately they were the same 8 hours !

I like the simple things in life !

Wow, you'll love my sister !

What time did your wristwatch stop ?

I don't know, I wasn't looking !

What do bees do when they move into a new hive ?

They have a house swarming party !
"Would you say your sister was pretty or ugly ?"

"Both!"

"How can she be both?"

"She's pretty ugly!"

A gorilla went into a quiet country restaurant, and ordered a cup of tea.

He gave the waitress a £10 note and she, thinking that the gorilla was probably a bit stupid, gave the gorilla just £3 change.

"We don't get a lot of gorillas in here," she said.

"I'm not surprised," replied the gorilla, "when you charge £7 for a cup of tea!"

My teacher, Miss Smith, took up bodybuilding recently.

In fact, she did so well at it that she's now Mr Smith!

2 men talking in hospital...

"I see they've brought in another case of diarrhoea !"

"Well, let's hope it tastes better than the tea they usually give us at bedtime !"

Whenever I'm down in the dumps,
I buy myself some new clothes !

Ah ! So that's where you get them from !

Where is the easiest place
to find diamonds ?

In a pack of cards !

A policeman stopped a car
on the motorway.

**"Do you realise that you were driving at
90 miles an hour ?"**

"I can't have been, I only left my house 10 minutes ago !"

The opera singer's voice filled the hall
- and then emptied it !

Which knight designed tombs ?

Sir Cophagus !

Which famous artist invented fizzy drinks ?

Lemonado Da Vinci !

"Mum, please may we make mud pies ?"

**"Yes, dear, but remember to wash your hands before you
eat them !"**

First cat -Where do fleas go in the winter ?

Second cat -Search me !

Why do vampires like funerals ?

Because every shroud has a silver lining !

How do you keep an idiot entertained for hours on end ?

Which two letters are bad for your teeth ?

D K !

How do you keep an idiot entertained for hours on end ?

**Just give him a piece of paper with
'PLEASE TURN OVER' on both sides !**

"You're late for school again !"

"I sprained my ankle !"

"What a lame excuse !"

What happened to the naughty witch at school ?

She was ex – spelled !

What sport did Frankenstein's monster compete in ?

The Pole Volt !

What do you give a sick snake ?

Asp - rin !

"I got a puncture driving here today !"

"I told you to watch out for that fork in the road !"

What did the curtain say to the window ?

"I've got you covered !"

What did the big chimney say to the little chimney ?

"You're far too young to smoke !"

I could never be in the submarine service - I have to sleep with the windows open !

Dumb Dan was given the job of painting the college flag-pole, but he didn't know how to work out how much paint he would need .

"Lay it on the floor and measure it," suggested a friend.

"Don't be stupid," replied Dan, "I need to know the height not the length !"

Did you hear about the idiot who simply could not do decimals - for some reason he could never see the point !

Why are vampires good comedians ?

They have a biting wit !

Why did the idiot take his windows to the shop ?

He wanted them measuring for new curtains !

My dog is a real problem. He chases everything
and anything on a bike ! I don't know what to do !

Just take his bike away !

My dog saw a sign that said "wet paint",
and so he did just that !

Why are toilet seats so cheap at the moment ?

**I don't know. I suppose the bottom must have
dropped out of the market !**

SPACED OUT

Why do aliens eat cabbage and sprouts ?

It puts colour in their cheeks !

What do you call an alien with two heads ?

A two-headed alien !

What do aliens do with humans they find in space ships ?

**Put them in the larder – they keep
tinned food for emergencies !**

What should you do if you find a green alien ?

Wait until it's ripe !

What is a robots favourite food ?

Nuclear fission Microchips !

What do you get if you cross a student and an alien ?

Something from another universe - ity !

What do you get if you cross an alien and a hot drink ?

Gravi - tea !

An astronaut and a chimp were fired off into space.
the chimp opened its sealed orders and, as it read
them it started pushing buttons and programming the flight
computer. When the astronaut opened his sealed orders he
found only one sentence...

"Feed the chimp !"

How do aliens go fishing ?

With earthworms !

Why do aliens have seven
fingers on each hand ?

**Because otherwise they would
have two empty
fingers in each glove !**

Where do aliens live ?

In green houses !

What lights do aliens switch on every Saturday ?

Satellites !

What game do aliens play to while away
the hours in deep space ?

Moonopoly !

Where do alien children
go in the evenings ?

Rocket and Roll concerts !

What are wealthy aliens members of ?

The Jet Set !

What are wealthy aliens members of ?

Where do aliens go to study their GCSEs ?

High School (Very High School) !

Why do aliens never starve in space ?

**Because they always know where to find a
Mars, a Galaxy and a Milky Way !**

What do evil aliens eat for lunch ?

Beans on toast - (Human Beans on toast) !

Why are aliens good for the environment ?

Because they are green !

What do aliens have to do before they can drive a rocket
at twice the speed of light in deep space ?

Reverse it out of the garage !

What do you get if you cross a mummy and a spaceship ?

Tutankha - moon !

What do aliens call junk food?

Unidentified Frying Objects!

How do you know when
aliens are envious?

Easy – they turn green!

What sort of sweets do Martians eat?

Martian mallows!

Where do aliens go to study rocket science?

Mooniversity!

How do you know when an alien is homesick?

He just moons about all over the place!

What do you give a sick alien ?

Planetcetamol !

Which railway company employs ghosts ?

British Wail !

How do you contact someone who lives on Saturn ?

Give them a ring !

What is the quickest way to get an alien baby to sleep ?

Rocket !

Alien School Report

Music   He loves the Planet Suite by Holst !

Chemistry Blew off one of his heads making
               rocket fuel !

Martian   KLargin SCRung jlkfr TTTTugt KLMgg
               FRelOOmmMw~We TTrRaaakk !

Maths   Can count up to seventeen using the
               fingers on his left hand !

Space   Takes a bite out of the Milky Way
               every time he goes there on a school trip !

What do you call an alien girl band ?

The Space Girls !

What do you call a mad alien ?

A Lunar-tic !

What is the name of the planet inhabited by video recorders ?

Planet of the Tapes !

What ticket do you ask for to go there for a holiday ?

Return to the Planet of the Tapes !

What game do nasty aliens play with Earth spaceships ?

Shuttlecocks !

Which side of a spaceship passes
closest to the planets ?

The Outside !

Why did the impressionist crash through the ceiling ?

He was taking off a rocket taking off !

What does an alien gardener do with his hedges ?

Eclipse them every spring !

Why did the alien buy a pocket computer ?

So he could work out how many pockets he has !

How can you tell if a computer is disgruntled ?

It will have a chip on its shoulder !

How do you get directions in deep space ?

Askeroid !

Did you hear about the Martian who went to a plastic
surgeon for a face lift ?

**She wanted her face to look like a million dollars, so the
surgeon made it all green and crinkly !**

Where do aliens keep fish they capture
from other planets ?

In a planetarium !

Why did the alien school have no computers ?

Because someone ate all the apples !

What do evil aliens grind up to make a hot drink ?

Coffee beings !

Who thought up the series 'Star Trek'

Some bright Spock !

What do you call an alien who travels
through space on a ketchup bottle?

A flying saucer!

How does a Martian know he's attractive?

When bits of metal stick to him!

What time is it when astronauts are hungry?

Launch time!

Why did the attendant turn space ships
away from the lunar car park?

It was a full moon!

What do you call a sad space ship?

An unidentified crying object!

What do you call a space ship made from cow pats?

A Pooh F O!

Where do alien space ship pilots go to learn how to fly in the darkness of outer space?

Night school!

Why are alien gardeners so good ?

Because they have green fingers !

❦

What do alien children do on Halloween ?

They go from door to door dressed as humans !

❦

What do aliens go to watch at the cinema ?

Starzan

❦

What do you get if you cross an alien
with apair of gloves ?

Greem fingers !

How do you know if there is an alien in your house ?

There will be a spaceship parked in the garden !

How do you communicate with aliens out in deep space ?

You have to shout really loudly !

How do you tell if an alien is embarrassed ?

They blush - and their cheeks go purple !

What do you get if you cross a cricket ball and an alien ?

A bowling green !

How do you catch a Venusian mega mouse ?

In a Venusian mega mouse-trap !

What do you give a sick alien ?

Paracetamoons !

Where do aliens do their shopping ?

In a greengrocers !

Why do some aliens make
their space ships out of
twisted planks of wood ?

**So they can travel at
warp speed !**

Who is in love with the alien James Bond ?

Miss Mooneypenny !

Where do aliens go for holidays ?

Lanzarocket !

What do aliens put on their cakes ?

Mars - ipan !

Who is the alien's favourite robot
cartoon character ?

Tin - Tin !

What game do bored aliens play ?

Astro noughts and crosses !

Why was the robot rubbing its joints with a video?

Because it was a video of Grease!

What is a robot's favourite chocolate?

Whole Nut!

Which star is the most dangerous?

The shooting star!

Why didn't the Martian have his birthday
party on the moon?

There was no atmosphere!

What did the teacher give the alien monster for lunch ?

Class 4B !

What sort of music do robots like best ?

Steel band music !

When the alien picked up his brand new
spaceship he was really pleased –
he'd never had a *NEW FO* before !

What do you give a robot who fancies a light snack ?

Some 60 watt bulbs !

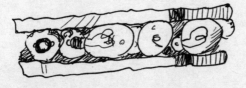

Why did the spaceship land outside your bedroom ?

I must have left the landing light on !

How do you know when a robot
has been in your fridge ?

There are footprints in the butter !

How do you invite a robot to a party ?

Send round a tinvitation !

What firework do aliens like best ?

Rockets !

What is the first thing an alien puts on when he
gets out of bed ?

His feet - ON - the floor !

Human - Why have you got holes in your hand ?

Alien - I ahve been using the computer.

Human - But that's not dangerous !

Alien - Maybe not on Earth, but on my planet when we talk about computer bytes we mean something different !

What do you call computer controlled sandpaper ?

Science Friction !

What is an alien's favourite TV programme ?

Blind date - it's the only way they can get a human girlfriend !

If you get lost in space - who should
you ask for directions ?

**An alien hairdresser -
they know all the short cuts !**

If an alien leaves his chewing gum orbiting
the Earth - what
do you call it ?

A Chew - F - O !

Your son will make an
excellent rocket pilot !

Why do you say that ?

**He has nothing but
space between his ears !**

Knock, knock...
Who's there ?
Saturn.
Saturn who ?
**Saturn front of this spaceship
waiting for take off time !**

What do daleks drink ?

Exterminade !

What do aliens put on their toast ?

Mars - malade !

Where is the smelliest part of an alien spaceship ?

The Com - poooh - ter !

Why do steel robots have so many friends ?

I suppose they must have magnetic personalities !

Why did the alien paint his spaceship
with sugar and vinegar?

He wanted a sweet and sour saucer!

How do you tip an alien spaceship over?

Rocket!

What did the greedy alien say when he
landed on a new planet?

Take me to your larder!

What dance can you see in the night sky ?

The Moon Walk !

Why did the football manager want to get
in touch with the alien ?

Because he knew where all the shooting stars were !

What did the mummy robot say to her children ?

Look before you bleep !

Why was the young robot so happy ?

Because he didn't have a chip on his shoulder !

Where does the alien gardener keep his tools?

In an astro - hut!

Where do Martians go to see a movie?

Cine - mars!

Knock, knock,
Who's there?
Jupiter
Jupiter Who?
Jupiter spaceship on my lawn?

SPACED OUT

What is worse than finding a 12 legged Venusian
mega - maggot in your apple ?

**Finding half a 12 legged Venusian
mega - maggot in your apple !**

What did the referee book the alien for ?

Hand ball, Hand ball, Hand ball, Hand ball....

What do aliens use to go up and down ?

Stairs !

Where did they put the alien who stole a field
full of rhubarb ?

In Custardy !

Ø

What is green and very noisy ?

An alien with a drum kit !

Ø

Who was the first man on the moon ?

A Spaceman !

Ø

What do you call a nosiy spaceship ?

A space racket !

Why do astronauts never eat after take off ?

Because they have just had a big launch !

What did one rocket say to the other ?

I wish I could stop smoking !

I don't know what to buy my pal, the
space alien, for his birthday ?

How about 5 pairs of slippers !

Why couldn't the idiot's spaceship travel
at the speed of light ?

Because he took off in the dark !

Where do you leave your spaceship whilst you visit another
planet ?

At a parking meteor !

Dis you hear about the alien poetess –
she wrote universes !

Why did the alien build a spaceship from feathers ?

He wanted to travel light years !

What do alien footballers wear when
they arrive on earth ?

Their landing strip !

NUTTY NOTIONS

What is furry and smells of mint ?

A Polo bear !

What do sparrows eat for breakfast ?

Tweet a Bix !

What do cats eat for breakfast ?

Shredded Tweet !

What does Doctor Jeckyll do on hoilday ?

He tans his Hyde !

How does the idiot call his dog ?

He puts both fingers in his mouth,
takes a deep breath and shouts here boy !

Which Russian leader was round and purple ?

Alexander the Grape !

What will you get if you swallow plutonium ?

Atomic ache !

What is a bunsen burner for ?

Setting fire to bunsens ?

Why is a real dog better than a cyberpet ?

Because your teacher will never believe you if you tell him that your cyberpet buried your homework in the back garden !

Why did the boy go to boarding school ?

Because he was always bored !

✎

"Have you put some more water in the goldfish bowl ?"

**"No, it hasn't drunk the water I put in
6 months ago yet !"**

✎

"Blenkinsop, you've been coming to my piano lessons for 6
months now, and I think it's time I told you – you aren't
supposed to blow it !"

✎

**He is the sort of man that girls look at twice – they can't
believe he is so ugly the first time !**

✎

How does an idiot get to the top of a tree ?

Stands on an acorn and waits for it to grow !

What do frogs drink at bedtime?

Croako!

Do old bicycles get recycled?

Do old car tyres get retired?

Why was the little girl wrapped up in bandages?

Because she was mummy's little pet!

Why was the fish so happy?

Because he was moving to a new plaice!

What do baby fish eat on their birthday?

Fish cakes!

What do gnomes eat at birthday parties?

Fairy cakes!

Who is the strongest man in the world?

**A policeman – he can hold up a whole streetful
of traffic with one hand!**

What should you never do when you see a dentist?

Take your cap off!

What is the name of the detective that Shakespeare
invented?

Shylock Holmes!

What do you call a bear without a beard ?

A bare faced bear !

What happened when the piano fell on the army barracks ?

There was A flat Major !

What time is it when you're hungry ?

Time for something to eat !

What came between the Iron Age and the Stone Age ?

The cabbage ?

What do you call a mad squirrel ?

Nuts !

What did the rabbit say when it went bald ?

Hare today, gone tomorrow !

What does a girl say when she's going out
with a bear ?

We're going teddy !

How can you send a liquid through the post
in an ordinary letter ?

When it's T !

What do you call somone who steals sheep ?

A Ram Raider !

What is big and grey and wobbly ?

A jellyphant !

Why was the pop group thrown out of the
nightclub by the bouncer ?

They were an elastic band !

What wears a sock on its bottom ?

Your leg !

Why was the idiot feeding his chickens haggis ?

He wanted them to lay Scotch eggs !

What is the only thing you can have in
an empty pocket ?

A Hole !

What sort of music do very, very cold
people listen to ?

The Blues !

"A robber, who stole three thousand bars of soap,
has made a clean getaway !"

Waiter – there's a dead mouse in my salad !

**It's the rubbish food in this place that
kills them, sir !**

Why did the elephant refuse to play cards
with his two friends ?

**Because one of them was lion and the other
was a cheetah !**

Waiter – what are these two worms on my plate ?

They are the sausages, sir !

How do you stop moles from digging up your lawn ?

Lock the toolshed !

What's black and white, and wet at the bottom ?

A nun paddling in the sea !

What do you call a fish with four eyes ?

Fiiiish !

Why are ducks so miserable ?

They always have down in the mouth !

What goes oom, oom, oom ?

A cow walking backwards !

Why do bees buzz ?

Because they can never remember the words !

What sort of crossword clues does Dracula like ?

Cryptic ones !

How does the queen of the sea travel around
her kingdom ?

By Octobus !

Mary had a little lamb,
She ate it with mint sauce !
If she buys a jar of mustard,
I'd watch out, mister horse !

How do you make a sausage roll ?

Push it down a steep hill !

Did you hear about the stupid farmer who took
his cows to the North Pole, thinking he
would get ice cream !

What do you get if you cross a skunk with a
hot air balloon ?

Something that stinks to high heaven !

Waiter – there's half a dead cockroach in my food!

You'll have to pay for the half you've eaten, Sir!

What sort of toys are rude?

Teddies – because they go around bear!

Why was the ugly monster called Isaiah?

Because one eye's higher than the other!

Look at those 50 cows over there!

I said, look at those 50 cows over there!!

Yes, I herd!

Why is the leopard the only animal that can't hide from hunters ?

Because it's always spotted !

What sort of dog is good at looking after children ?

A Baby Setter

How do you know when a dog is house-trained ?

It leaves its little poodles outside !

What do monsters eat for breakfast ?

Lice Crispies !

4 kippers please, and leave the eyes in
– I'll need something to see me through the week !

Where are school dinners served ?

The Mushroom !

With alphabet soup,
you can spell your name,
you can write rude words,
again and again.
With alphabet soup,
take it or leave it,
whatever you spell,
you know you'll have to eat it !

How do you survive an electric shock ?

Call the operator and ask them to reverse the charge !

What sort of bird can see round corners ?

A Crane !

A young man was sitting by the fire watching
the kettle boil...

"If only we could harness this wonderful power of steam,
perhaps one day we could even use it to drive vehicles and
carry people from one town to another..."

His mother called out to him...

"Hurry up and get dressed or you'll miss the train to work
again!"

Where is the best place to keep a pie?

Your tummy!

When do kangaroos propose?

In Leap Years!

What building drips cheese and tomatoes
onto the town beneath ?

The leaning tower of Pizza !

Why couldn't Noah, his son and his wife all go fishing ?

He only had two worms !

Did you hear about the orchestra leader who
survived being hit by lightning ?

Fortunately he was a very bad conductor !

What is green and hot and goes
round and round ?

An alien in a tumble drier !

Why are babies so good at football ?

**Because they know how to dribble from the moment they
are born !**

Did you hear about the stupid robber?

He threw a brick through the jewellers
window on Monday night, and then came back
and did the same again on Tuesday night
– someone told him that the window
had double glazing!

What are round and pink and wear trainers?

Jogging bottoms!

Doctor, doctor, my wife thinks she's a jumbo jet!

Don't be silly – she isn't even an elephant!

What do bad comedians eat at breakfast ?

Corny flakes !

Why did the alien turn the restaurant waiter
upside down ?

Someone told him that you had to tip the waiter !

Why did the witch put her broomstick in the fridge ?

She fancied a cold spell !

Which holiday camp do goats go to ?

Buttlins !

What do you say to a hitch-hiking frog ?

Hop In !

What do you get if you cross a cow
and a kangaroo ?

Something you need a trampoline to milk !

Where do policemen go on holiday ?

The Copper Cobana Beach !

How do fish go on holiday ?

By Whale way !

How do cavemen get to know each other ?

By joining clubs !

What do you call frozen mice ?

Micicles !

What is a shark's favourite pudding?

**Spotted Dick - so if you are called Dick, make
sure they don't spot you!**

Doctor, doctor, my little boy has swallowed
my wristwatch!

Don't worry, we will soon see the passage of time!

What do idiot's have for pudding?

Clotted Dick!

What did the woman say to the masked man
working in her local bank?

I'd like to see the loan arranger, Lone Ranger!

Why do posties like Z?

Because there aren't any more letters after it!

What did the maths teacher do when his
nose got blocked ?

He worked it out with his pencil and ruler !

How do you keep an idiot in suspense ?

I'll tell you on page 2,890 !

What does an elephant do when it has diarrhoea ?

Goes to the toilet !

What did the sheep say to his girlfriend ?

I: love ewe !

What do you call a wizard on a broomstick ?

A Flying Sorcerer !

What exams are gardeners good at ?

Hoe levels !

What exams are Santa's good at ?

Ho, Ho, Ho levels !

Why were the carpenter's teeth chipped ?

Because he was always biting his nails !

What is a jelly baby's favourite sweet ?

Chewing gum !

What did the vampire doctor say ?

Necks please !

Two oranges were playing tennis - it was 40 all
- what did the umpire shout ?

Juice !

Why does Dracula never intend to get married ?

He is a bat - chelor !

What happened to the football that was
kicked close to a fan ?

It blew out of the stadium !

What sort of car does an alligator drive ?

Some old crock !

What job did the spider get ?

A web designer !

What do you get if you cross a warlock and a PC ?

A computer wizard !

What do you get if you cross a dinosaur with a fish ?

Jurassic shark !

What does an Italian pirate's parrot say ?

Pizzas of eight, pizzas of eight !

When Mary had a little lamb,
the doctor was surprised,
but when Old Macdonald had a farm,
he *just* couldn't believe his eyes !

Little Jack Horner,
sat in the corner,
eating his Christmas pie.
Along came a spider,
and sat down beside him,
and said "I think I'm in the wrong poem here !"

What do cannibals do at a wedding ?

Toast the bridesmaids !

What sort of jungle animal works on the railways ?

A railway lion !

What is the best time of year to pick
apples and pears ?

**Summer – that's when the farmer is
away on holiday !**

What pen does a hairless man use ?

A bald point !

Where are you allowed to eat toffees ?

On a chew – chew train !

Where do cats sleep ?

On a caterpillar !

Why should you always laugh when a vampire
tells you a joke ?

Because they like people to get the point !

❧

What sort of posters do naughty teddies find
themselves on ?

Wan = Ted posters !

❧

What do you get out of a poorly piano ?

A sick note !

❧

What has a bottom at the top ?

Your legs !

What does Tarzan eat ?

Fish and chimps !

Where does Tarzan buy his clothes ?

At a jungle sale !

Where does Tarzan the vampire bite people ?

In the Jungular !

What were Tarzan's last words ?

"Who put grease on that vine...?"

Where does Tarzan buy his loincloths ?

From an end of loin sale !

What did the man say when he walked into the bar ?

OOF ! (It was metal bar !)

What can't pigs ever get a good radio or TV signal ?

There's always too much cracklin !

What do you find in an angry sewing machine ?

Cross stitches !

Why did the idiot come top of the class at school ?

He was the only one who passed the dope test !

What fish went to music college ?

The piano tuna !

What sound does a Chinese frog make ?

Where do footballers go dancing?

At a foot - ball !

They make a perfect couple - He has a chip on his shouder, and there's something fishy about her !

What sound does a Chinese frog make ?

Cloak !

Where does a six foot parrot sleep ?

Wherever it wants to !

Is that a bulldog ?

No, it's a Labrador, but it ran into a wall
chasing a cat !

What sort of dog has no tail ?

A hot dog !

Why did the idiot throw a bucket of water
into the wardrobe ?

Someone told him there was a smoking
jacket in there !

What sort of vampires are interested in sport ?

Football fangs !

How did the skeleton escape being eaten by a dog ?

It was a marrow escape !

Why is the school orchestra in China?

Because they made the mistake of asking if the audience had any requests!

What is white, scary and soft?

A jellyton!

What is white, scary and swims round in the sea?

A skellyfish!

Why is the man with the photographic memory so miserable?

He has negative thoughts!

What's black and white and red ?

A zebra with nappy rash !

There's a stick insect in my salad - fetch me the branch manager at once !

How do you eat your turkey dinner ?

I just gobble it down !

Waiter, waiter, there's a button in my lettuce !

Ah ! That will be from the salad dressing sir !

How do you find a lost dog ?

Make a sound like a bone !

What weighs two and a half tons, is grey, and floats gracefully through the air ?

A Hang Gliding Elephant !

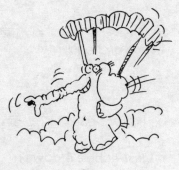

What's the worst thing about being a millipede ?

Washing your hands before tea !

What did the earwig sing as it went to a football match ?

Earwig - go, earwig - go, earwig - go....

What do you call an 85 year old ant ?

An antique !

What is worse than
finding a slug in
your salad
sandwich ?

Finding half a slug !

what did King Kong say when he
was told that his sister had had
a baby ?

I'll be a monkey's uncle !

A man slipped when working on his roof, and was hanging
onto the window ledge by his fingertips. he saw the cat
through the window and called out to it to get help.

The cat said 'me ? how ?'

What do cats read in the morning ?

The Mewspapaer !

What happens when there is a stampede
of cows on the motorway?

There is udder chaos!

Where do you keep a pet vampire fish?

In your blood stream!

Have you ever hunted bear?

No, it's far too cold in this part of the world for that!

A cat just scratched my leg!

Shall I put some cream on it?

No, it will be miles away by now!

What is grey, has a trunk and travels at
125 miles an hour ?

A businessman on a fast train !

How did your budgie die ?

Flu !

Don't be daft, budgies
can't die from flu !

**This one did – it flu
under a steam roller !**

What is big and grey and has yellow feet ?

An elephant standing in custard !

What fish can you
see in the sky ?

A Starfish !

Where do kippers go to be cured ?

They go to the local sturgeon !

Waiter - this crab only has one claw
!

Sorry, sir, it must have been in a fight !

**In that case, take this away and bring me
the winner !**

Doctor, doctor, I think I'm a cat !

How long have you felt like this ?

Since I was a kitten !

What time is it when an elephant sits on your fence ?

Time to get a new fence !

What does it mean if your nose starts to run ?

It's trying to catch a cold !

What do you call a worm in a fur coat ?

A caterpillar !

Help, I've lost my cat !

Well, why don't you put an advert in the local newspaper ?

Don't be silly – cats can't read !

Eric, what is a prickly pear ?

Er....two porcupines ?

Why do crabs walk sideways ?

**Because they had to take some medicine
which had side effects !**

What sort of insects don't know the words
to songs ?

Hum bugs !

A frog went to the doctor with a sore throat,
the doctor examined him and said..."you've got
a person in your throat !"

Where do ducks keep their savings?

In river banks!

My dog often goes for a tramp in the woods - and the
tramp is getting a bit fed up with it!

What is the easiest way to get an elephant
to follow you home?

Just act like a nut!

What do you call a dog that thinks it's a sheep?

Baaaaaking mad!

What went into the lion's cage at the zoo and came out without a scratch ?

Another lion !

When do lorry drivers stop for a snack ?

When they see a fork in the road !

How do chimps make toast ?

Put it under a gorilla !

What is grey and highly dangerous ?

An elephant with a hand grenade !

IN SICKNESS AND
IN HEALTH

Why did the angry doctor have to retire ?

Because he had lost all his patients !

Doctor, doctor...
I think I've got an inferiority comlex !

No you haven't you really are inferior !

Ah. Mr Smith, have your eyes ever been checked ?

No doctor, they've always been blue !

Nurse – Can you take this patient's temperature please.

Certainly doctor – where to ?

Doctor, I can't get to sleep at night !

Sleep on a window sill – you'll soon drop off !

Doctor, doctor...
There's a man to see you with a wooden leg
called Jenkins.

What's his other leg called ?

Doctor, doctor.
I think I'm turning into a wasp !

**Hmm, give me a buzz if things get
really bad !**

Doctor, doctor.
I've just been stung by a wasp !

Did you put anything on it ?

**No, he seemed to enjoy it just
as it was !**

Doctor, doctor..
I've got an itchy, spotty patch on my nose.
Should I put cream on it ?

Now, now let's not do anything rash !

Doctor, doctor..
I've not stopped laughing since my operation !

Well, I told you the surgeon would have you in stitches !

Doctor, doctor..
I've got pigeon toes !

**Don't worry, we'll find a suitable tweetment for you..but
for now just put this birdseed in your shoes !**

Doctor, doctor..
Which Kings needed medical attention ?

**Charles the Sick
and
Henry the ache**

✎

DOCTOR'S BOOKCASE..

Training to be a surgeon
by
I Cuttem Open

✎

Doctor are you sure its my arteries that are the problem ?

Liste, I'm a doctor, aorta know !

✎

Doctor, doctor..
Thank you for coming – I'm at death's door !

Don't worry, I'll pull you through !

Doctor, doctor,
I feel like a twenty pound note !

Go shopping, the change will do you good !

Doctor, doctor.
I can't stop shoplifting !

**Try taking two of these pills every morning and if that
doesn't work bring me a CD player next week !**

Did you hear about the appendix who went out and
bought a new suit - because he heard that the doctor
was going to take him out !

Doctor, doctor.
Which King was also a doctor ?

William the corn curer !

Doctor, doctor...
Is it true that you can get pills to improve your memory?

Of course you can, how many would you like?

How many what?!

My belly is so big I'm embarrassed by it!

have you tried to diet?

Yes, but whatever colour I use it still sticks out!

Doctor, doctor...
I feel as sick as a dog!

I'll make an appintment for you to see a vet!

Doctor, doctor,.
I keep thinking I'm a big bar of chocolate !

**Come and sit here and don't worry I won't bite –
I'm just a big old pussycat really !**

Doctor, doctor,.
I've got a terrible cough !

Well you should practice more !

Doctor, doctor,.
After the operation on my hand, will I be
able to play the piano ?

Of course you will Mr Smith !

Great – because I never could before !

Doctor, doctor.
I have an inferiority complex !

Hmm. Not a very big one is it !

✎

Doctor, doctor.
I think I'm a cat !

How long have you felt like this ?

Since I was a kitten !

✎

Doctor, doctor.
I feel like a goat !

Really - how are the kids !

✎

Doctor, doctor.
I think I'm turning into a bridge !

Really - what's come over you !

Doctor, doctor..
Why did the chemist tell everyone to be quiet?

Because she didn't want to wake the sleeping pills!

Doctor, doctor..
I think I'm turning into a fish!

Well, just hop on the scales!

Doctor, doctor..
These tablets you gave me last week seem
to get smaller every day!

Yes, they're slimming pills!

Doctor, doctor..
I think I'm turning into a toad !

**Don't worry, we can do an hoperation
for that these days !**

Doctor, doctor..
can you put me in touch with the local
plastic surgeon ?

**I'm afraid not, he sat too close to the radiator
last night and melted !**

Ah Mr Blenkinsop. Did you drink the medicine I gave you
after your bath ?

**No, doctor, I couldn't even drink all the bath water,
let alone the medicine !**

Doctor, doctor.
I have a fish hook stuck in the side of my mouth !

**I thought you were waiting to see me
with baited breath!**

Doctor, doctor.
I've just been stung by a giant wasp !

I'll give you some cream to put on it !

Don't be daft – it'll be miles away by now !

Doctor, doctor.
My new job at the laundry is very tiring !

I thought you looked washed out !

Doctor, doctor.
I feel quite like my old self again !

Oh dear, I'd better put you back on the tablets then !

Doctor, doctor.
I get a lot of headaches from my wooden leg !

Why's that ?

My wife keeps hitting me over the head with it !

Doctor, doctor.
I got trampled by a load of cows !

So I herd !

Doctor, doctor.
I keep imagining I'm a sunken ship and its
really got me worried !

Sounds to me like you're a nervous wreck !

Doctor, doctor..
My snoring wakes me up every night !

**Try sleeping in another bedroom, then you won't
be able to hear it !**

Doctor, doctor..
I think I have a split personality !

I'd better give you a second opinion then !

Doctor, doctor..
What can you give me for my kidneys ?

How about a pound of onions ? !

Doctor, doctor..
I've fractured my elbow bone !

Humerus ?

Well, I don't think it's particu;larly funny !

✎

Doctor, doctor..
My hair is falling out – can you give me
something to keep it in !

Here's a paper bag !

✎

Doctor, doctor..
My wife thinks I'm a hypochondriac

Why haven't you been to see me before about this ?

I've been too ill !

Doctor, doctor.
Is this disease contagious ?

Not at all !

Then why are you standing out on the window ledge ?!

Doctor, doctor.
You don't really think I'm turning into a grandfather clock
do you ?

No, I was just winding you up !

Doctor, doctor.
My son is turning into a cricket bat !

Hmm! Well this has got me stumped !

Doctor, doctor..
I think I'm a crocodile !

Don't worry, you'll soon snap out of it !

✎

Doctor, doctor..
I think I've just swallowed a chicken bone !

Are you choking ?

No, I'm serious !

✎

'I'm sorry Mr Smith, but I think you have rabies!"

"In that case give me a piece of paper and a pen."

"Are you going to write your will ?"

"No, a list of people I want to bite !"

✎

Doctor, doctor..
I think I have acute appendicitis!

Yes, it is rather nice isn't it !

Doctor – Put your tongue out and say Aaaah, please!

Patient – Aaaaah!

Doctor – Yuck! You're not going to put that thing back in your mouth are you!

✏

I thought you said he was a vet – he knows nothing about animal medicine at all!

I didn't say he was a vet – I said he had a sore throat – he's a hoarse doctor!

✏

Why do surgeons wear masks?

So that no-one will know who it was if they make a mistake!

143692

What do you call an American dentist?

A Yank!

✏

Doctor, doctor...
My wife thinks she's a door!

I think she's just a bit unhinged!

✏

Doctor, doctor,
I've got a button stuck up my nose,
what should I do?

Breathe through the 4 little holes!

✏

"Blenkinsop - you asked for the afternoon off
yesterday to go and see your doctor.

Yet I saw you going into a football match
with a friend!"

"The doctor is my friend!"

My son has just been accepted by a medical school –
but they don't want him while he's alive !

Doctor, doctor.
What can I do to help me get to sleep ?

Have you tried counting sheep ?

Yes, but then I have to wake up to drive home again !

Doctor, doctor.
I think I'm a dog !

Well take a seat and I'll have a look at you !

I can't – I'm not allowed on the furniture !

WHAT DO YOU CALL...

What do you call a person made of rubber who stands by
the door of a nightclub ?

A Bouncer !

What do you call a vampire singer ?

Fang Sinatra !

What two fish swim across the bed of a lake at
90 miles an hour ?

A Motor Pike and Side Carp !

What do you call a man with a motorcycle
hat on in Germany ?

Helmut !

What do you call the river that starred in a
cowboy film ?

The Magnificent Severn !

What do you call a woman who juggles pints of beer in a pub ?

Beertrix !

What do you call a bird that goes to college ?

Polly technic !

What do you call a rodent's favourite meal ?

Ratatouille !

What do you call a singing fish ?

A sole singer !

What do you call a woman with a
parrot on her head?

Polly!

What do you call a woman who works
as a bodyguard?

Sal a minder!

What do you call a man with a sack, a long
white beard and a sleigh?

Bjorn, the oldest postman in Iceland!

What do you call a monkey who is king of the jungle?

Henry the Ape!

What do you call a woman with a shotgun in her hand?

Whatever she tells you to, or else!

What do you call a man who lives just around
the corner?

That's Andy!

What do you call a duck that lives in a teapot?

A Quackpot!

What do you call a pony with a sore throat?

A Little Hoarse!

What do you call a rodent with a sword?

A Mouseketeer!

What do you call a woman with a white face?

Blanche!

What do you call a sloth's favourite drink ?

Ice cream slowda !

What do you call a woman with two horses ?

Gi - Gi !

What do you call a smelly giant gorilla ?

King Pong !

What do you call a posh car for butchers ?

A Sausage Rolls !

What do you call a dog that likes doing puzzles ?

A lab-rynth !

(An amazing breed !)

What do you call a man who never pays
for his food ?

Bill !

What do you call a Roman leader with a cold ?

Julius Sneezer !

What do you call a man who owns a
seaside sweet factory ?

Rock !

What do you call a machine that works out
how many pockets you have ?

A Pocket Calculator !

What do you call a snake with a
pocket calculator ?

An Adder !

What do you call a pig with fangs ?

A hampire !

What do you call a pig that acts in Shakespeare plays ?

Hamlet !

What do you call the jewels that ghosts wear ?

Tomb stones !

What do you call a woman who was eaten
by her cannibal husband ?

Henrietta !

What do you call a woman who has lots of men at her feet ?

A chiropodist !

What do you call the eating implements used by karate club members ?

Chop sticks !

What do you call a mushroom who has lots of fun at parties ?

A Fungi !

What do you call a vicar on a motorbike ?

Rev !

What do you call the instruments made from people's insides that monsters play ?

Organs !

What do you call a man with a clock in the shape
of the moon ?

A Lunartick !

What do you get if you cross a chicken with a dog ?

Pooched eggs !

What do you call an elephant crossed with an insect ?

Forget - me - gnat !

What do you call keep fit for ghosts ?

Exorcise !

What do you call an ancient Egyptian who's crumbling ?

A Crummy Mummy !

What do you call a dog that can operate a
farmer's 4 wheel drive?

A Land Rover!

What do you call a ghostly teddy bear?

Haunted!

What do you call a pale teddy bear?

Wanted!

What do you call a woman who knows where she lives?

Olivia!

What do you call a sun tanned teddy bear?

Unwanted!

What do you call a rock climbing teddy bear?

Mounted!

What do you call a teddy bear that's been knocked down
by a car?

Dented!

What do you call a sweet smelling teddy bear?

Scented!

What do you call a happy teddy bear ?

Contented !

What do you call a teddy bear left at the altar ?

Jilted !

What do you call a teddy bear that serves in
Parliament ?

Elected !

What do you call Long John Silver's younger brother ?

Short John Silver !

What does a whale call the youngest
member of the family ?

Her baby blubber !

What do you call two rows of cabbages ?

A dual cabbageway !

What do you call a worm rich enough to buy a
fur jacket ?

A Caterpillar !

What do you call a wig for a rabbit ?

A Harepiece !

What do you call a popular woman who stays
out in the sun for far too long ?

The Toast Of The Town !

What do you call a man with a police car on his head ?

Nick, nick, nick !

What do you call the person who delivers mail to
a football club ?

The goal-post-man !

What do you call a man with a heavy goods
vehicle on his head

Laurie !

What do you call an Owl that robs the rich and gives to
the poor ?

Robin Hoot !

What do you call a Scottish lunchtime assistant ?

Dinner Ken !

What do you call a Scotsman who knows everything ?

Ken !

What do you call a hippo at the South Pole ?

Lost !

What do you call the stuff that space aliens
put on their cakes ?

Star - zipan !

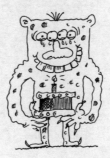

What do you call a play acted by ghosts ?

A Phantomime !

What do you call a homeless snail ?

A slug !

What do you call a Welsh comedian ?

Dai Laughing !

What do you call the very earliest spaceship ?

A Dinosaucer !

What do you call the woman who fell off the cliff ?

Eileen Dover !

What do you call the man walking on dried leaves ?

Russell !

What do you call a man who can't swim?

Bob!

What do you call a woman who walks around lost?

Wanda!

What do you call a vegetable that goes camping?

A boy sprout!

What do you call a film about wildfowl?

A Duckumentary!

What do you call the job of making nun's clothes?

Habit forming!

What do you call a a lorry full of feet ?

A toe truck !

What do you call a snake that crushes wild pigs ?

A boar constrictor !

What do you call an older member of your family who thinks he's a pen ?

Your Bic brother !

What do you call an embarrassed potato ?

A beetroot !

What do you call a vampire's favourite pudding ?

Leeches and Scream !

What do you call a goat's favourite food ?

Alphabutt soup !

What do you call a cross between a dog and a phone ?

A Golden Receiver !

What do you call the place where baby monkeys sleep ?

An Apricot !

What do you call a buffalo that you can wash
your hands in ?

A Bison !

What do you call a failed magician's relative?

His Half-brother!

What do you call a deer that goes out in bad weather?

A Rain-deer!

What do you call a place where cats and dogs
go to get new tails?

A Retailer!

What do you call a bird that loves to play cowboys?

Wyatt Chirp!

What do you call a horse that a monster eats at 3 a.m.?

A Nightmare!

What do you call a common alien dog ?

A Moon-grel !

What do you call the leader of a convent who conquers the World ?

Attila the Nun !

What do you call a Russian gardener ?

Ivanhoe !

What do you call a dog that is always rushing around ?

A dash - hound !

What do you call the flying machines invented
by mummies ?

Pharaohplanes !

What do you call the event that undertakers and
their ponies go to each year ?

The Hearse of the Year Show !

What do you call the method of transport used
on the sea bed ?

Taxi-crab !

What do you call it when cannibals eat a comedian ?

A feast of fun !

What do you call a dog that keeps making a bolt
for the door ?

Blacksmith !

What do you call a place where you can
rent out Dracula ?

Vamp-Hire !

What do you call a noisy alien party ?

A Space Racket !

What do you call the first part of a robot
teacher's schoolday ?

Assembly !

What do you call a man who delivers christmas
presents to lions and tigers ?

Santa Claws !

What do you call it when a Chinese man visits his dentist ?

Tooth Hurty !

What do you call a man who steals things ?

Rob !

What do you call a burglar who fell in a cement mixer ?

A Hardened Criminal !

What do you call the bird that brings monster babies ?

Frankenstork !

What do you call a frog that allows you to park your car ?

A Parking Kermit !

What do you call a short legged tramp ?

A Low Down Bum !

What do you call it when you flush a lot ?

A Chain Reaction !

What do you call a pig driving a car ?

Road hog !

What do you call a TV programme set
round a breakfast table ?

A Cereal !

What do you call something with 8 legs and
a terrible voice ?

The School Choir !

What do you call the barrell of beer that fell on a man without hurting him?

Light Ale!

What do you call a cat that chases outlaws?

Posse!

What do you call the place where cats get on the coach?

The Puss Stop!

What do you call a lazy man in a bakery?

A Loafer!

What do you call a dad who sits in the freezer ?

An Ice Cold Pop !

What do you call a woman who spends all her
time in the bookmakers ?

Bette !

What do you call it when you shoot at the
alarm clock ?

Killing Time !

What do you call a car that acts in adventure films ?

Harrison Ford !

What do you call the worst player in the
school football team ?

The Drawback !

What do you call the nuts that fly around in space?

Astronuts!

What do you call the place where ghosts go for their holidays?

The Isle of Fright!

What do you call a crocodile's favourite card game?

Snap!

What do you call a baby crab?

A Nipper!

What do you call the ghost that is a member of the Royal family?

The Prince of Wails!

What do you call a liquid that can never freeze?

Hot Water!

What do you call an adventurous skeleton?

Indiana Bones!

What do you call the teacher with no legs,
arms or body?

The Head!

What do you call a man with a seagull on his
head and sand at his feet?

Cliff!

What do you call a man whose father was a Canon?

A Son of a Gun!

What do you call a man with two left feet?

**Whatever you like - if he tries to catch you
he'll just run round in circles!**

What did the Spaniard call his first and only son?

Juan!

What do you call a Scotsman with a computer on his head?

Mac!

What do you call a
weekly television
programme about
people getting
washed ?

A Soap Opera !

What do you call a
flock of birds who
fly in formation ?

The Red Sparrows !

What do you call a bee who is always complaining ?

A Grumble Bee !

What would you call a friend who had an elephant
on his head ?

A Flatmate !

What do you call a song played on car horns ?

A Car Tune !

What do you call the man who invented a famous car and toilet paper ?

Lou Rolls !

What do you call an elephant that has had too much to drink ?

Trunk !

What do you call a woman who works at the zoo ?

Ellie Fant !

What do you call
the owner of a tool
factory?

The Vice Chairman!

What do you call
King Midas when
he stars in a James
Bond film?

Goldfinger!

What do you call a
parrot when it has
dried itself after a
bath?

Polly Unsaturated!

What do you call a dentist in the army?

A Drill Sergeant!

What do you call a Kangaroo at the North Pole ?

A Lost - Tralien !

What do you call a rabbit dressed up as a cake ?

A Cream Bun !

What do you call the illness that martial arts experts suffer from ?

Kung Flu !

What do you call a woman whoplays snooker with a pint of beer on her head ?

Beatrix Potter !

What do you call the man who went to a fancy dress party
as a sandwich ?

Roland Butter !

What do you call a man who rescues drowning
spooks from the sea ?

A Ghost Guard !

What do you call someone who makes half size
models of fish ?

A Scale Modeller !

What do you call someone with a male cat on his head ?

Tom !

What do you call someone who draws funny
pictures of motor vehicles ?

A Car - Toonist !

What do you call someone who dances on cars ?

A Morris Dancer !

What do you call a fight between film actors ?

Star Wars !

What do you call a girl who comes out
very early in the morning ?

Dawn !

What do you call a group of cars ?

A Clutch !

What do you call a puzzle that is so hard it
makes people swear ?

A Crossword !

What do you call a dog that is always getting
into fights ?

A Boxer !

What do you call a woman with a sinking
ship on her head ?

Mandy Lifeboats !

What do you call a witch's broomstick when
you are very young?

A Broom Broom!

What do you call a film about Mallards?

A Duckumentary!

What do you call a musical instrument that is
played by two teams of twenty people?

A Piano Forte!

What do you call a Scottish man with a castle on his head?

Fort William!

What do you call a very fast horse?

Gee Gee Whizz!

What do you call the best dad in the world?

Top of the Pops!

What do you call a chocolate that teases
small animals?

A Mole - teaser!

What do you call a fish on a motorcycle?

A Motor Pike!

What do you call a pen with no hair?

A Bald Point!

What do you call a thing with 22 legs,
11 heads and 2 wings ?

A Football Team !

What do you call a cow that cuts grass ?

A Lawn Moooooer !

What do you call a man with a box of
treasure on his head ?

Chester !

What do you call a magical secret agent ?

James Wand !

What do you call it when an aeroplane
disappears over the horizon ?

Boeing, Going, Gone !

What do you call a hearing aid made from fruit ?

A Lemonade !

PARDON ??

What do you call a girl with a head made of honey ?

Bee - trix !

What do you call a policeman with blonde hair ?

A Fair Cop !

What do you call a 5-a-side match played
by chimney sweeps ?

Soot Ball !

What do you call a small parent ?

A Minimum !

What do you call a man with legal documents on his head ?

Will !

What do you call a traffic warden who never
fines anyone ?

A Triffic Warden !

What do you call a telephone call from one
vicar to another ?

A Parson to Parson call !

What do you call the place where parrots
make films ?

PollyWood !

What do you call a girl with a head made of glass ?

Crystal !

What do you call a scared biscuit ?

A Cowardy Custard Cream !

What do you call an Igloo without a toilet ?

An Ig !

What do you call a superb painting done
by a rat ?

A Mouseterpiece !

What do you call a man with a jumbo jet
parked on his head ?

Ron Way !

What do you call a box of parrot food?

Polly Filla!

What do you call it when you pass out after
eating too much curry?

A Korma!

What do you call a chicken that eats cement?

A Bricklayer!

What do you call a dog that's always
snapping at people?

Camera!

CRAZY CROSSES

What do you get if you cross a sheep and a space ship ?

Apollo Neck Woolly Jumpers !

What do you get if you cross a pig
with a naked person ?

Streaky Bacon !

What do you get if you cross a box of
matches and a giant ?

The Big Match !

What do you get if you cross a naked woman
and the bottom of the ocean ?

A deep sea Lady Godiva !

What do you get if you cross a plumber with
a field of cow pats ?

The Poohed Piper !

What do you get if you cross an elephant
and a bottle of whisky ?

Trunk and Disorderly !

What do you get if you cross a flock
of sheep and a radiator ?

Central Bleating !

What do you get if you cross a singer and
a tall ladder ?

Someone who can easily get the high notes !

What do you get if you cross a skunk
and a pair of tennis rackets ?

Ping Pong !

What do you get if you cross a pudding
and a cow pat ?

A Smelly Jelly !

What do you get if you cross a pig and
a box of itching powder ?

Pork Scratching !

What do you get if you cross a jellyfish
and an aircraft ?

A jelly copter !

What do you get if you cross a bear with a freezer?

A teddy brrrrrr!

What do you get if you cross a computer with a vampire?

Something new fangled!

What do you get if you cross a vampire with a mummy?

Something you wouldn't want to unwrap!

What do you get if you cross a cow with a grass cutter?

A lawn mooer!

What do you get if you cross an
ice cream with a dog ?

Frost-bite !

What do you get if you cross a helicopter
with a cornish pasty ?

Something pie in the sky !

What do you get if you cross a carrier pigeon
with a woodpecker ?

A bird that knocks before delivering a message !

What do you get if you cross a frog
and a secret agent ?

A croak and dagger story !

What do you get if you cross a shoulder
bag with a Mallard ?

A Ducksack !

What do you get if you cross a dinosaur with a dog ?

Tyrannosaurus Rex !

What do you get if you cross a football team with a bunch
of crazy jokers ?

Mad Jester United !

What do you get if you cross a pig
and a telephone ?

A lot of crackling on the line !

What do you get if you cross a Viking
and a detective ?

Inspector Norse!

What do you get if you cross a large computer and a
beefburger ?

A Big Mac !

What do you get if
you cross an overheating
large computer with a
beefburger ?

A Big Mac and Fries !

What do you get if
you cross a hat factory
and a field of cows ?

A pat on the head !

What do you get if you cross a mouse
and a bottle of olive oil ?

A squeak that oils itself !

What do you get if you cross a jogger
with an apple pie ?

Puff pastry !

What do you get if you cross a detective with a cat ?

A Peeping Tom !

What do you get if you cross a
vampire and a plumber ?

A drain in the neck !

What do you get if you cross a TV programme
and a load of sheep ?

A flock-U-mentary !

What do you get if you cross a footballer
and a mythical creature ?

A centaur forward !

What do you get if you cross an actress and a
glove puppet ?

Sooty and Streep !

What do you get if you cross an
Italian landmark and a ghost ?

The screaming tower of Pisa !

What do you get if you cross a pasty
and a scary film ?

A Cornish Nasty !

What do you get if you cross a pig
and a part in a film ?

A Ham Roll !

What do you get if you cross a sports
reporter with a vegetable ?

A Common Tater !

What do you get if you cross a joke book
and a snowstorm ?

Corn Flakes !

What do you get if you cross a wireless with
a hairdresser ?

Radio waves !

What do you get if you cross a hairdresser
and a bucket of cement ?

Permanent waves !

What do you get if you cross a toadstool
and a full suitcase ?

Not mushroom for your holiday clothes !

What do you get if you cross a dog with a vampire ?

A were - woof !

What do you get if you cross a telephone
and a marriage bureau ?

A Wedding Ring !

What do you get if you cross a bike and a rose ?

Bicycle petals !

What do you get if you cross an alligator
and King Midas ?

A croc of gold !

What do you get if you cross a king and a boat ?

King Canoe !

What do you get if you cross a tortoise and a storm ?

An 'I'm not in a hurry cane !'

What do you get if you cross a chicken with a pod ?

Chick peas !

What do you get if you cross a computer
with a potato ?

Micro chips !

What do you get if you cross a herb and
Doctor Who ?

A Thyme Machine !

What do you get if you cross a dog with a maze ?

A labyrinth !

What do you get if you cross a cow with a crystal ball ?

A message from the udder side !

What do you get if you cross a
crocodile with a camera ?

A snapshot !

What do you get if you cross two sailors and a
bottle of HP ?

Tartare Sauce !

What do you get if you cross a chicken
and an electricity socket ?

A battery hen !

What do you get if you cross a plank of wood
and a pencil ?

A drawing board !

What do you get if
you cross a dog
with a football game ?

Spot-The-Ball !

What do you get if
you cross a spider
with a computer ?

A web page !

What do you get if you cross a sheep with
a holiday resort ?

The Baaahaaamaaas !

What do you get if you cross a frog
with a traffic warden ?

Toad away !

What do you get if you cross a flea
with some moon rock ?

A lunar - tick !

What do you get if you cross a jet engine
and a tennis racket ?

A Tennis Rocket !

What do you get if you cross a vampire
and a circus entertainer ?

Something that goes straight for the juggler !

What do you get if you cross a snake
with a building site ?

A boa-constructor !

What do you get if you cross an insect and a dance ?

A cricket ball !

What do you get if you cross a cake and a disco ?

Abundance !

What do you get if you cross a mountain
and a baby ?

A cry for Alp !

What do you get if you cross a
vampire and a bowl of soup ?

Scream of Tomato !

What do you get if you cross a pig and a laundry ?

Hogwash !

What do you get if you cross a bunch
of flowers with some insects ?

Ants in your plants !

What do you get if you cross a bunch of
flowers with a burgler ?

Robbery with violets !

What do you get if you cross a cow and a goat ?

Butter from a butter !

What do you get if you cross a pair of
hiking boots and a parrot ?

A walkie-talkie !

What do you get if you cross a bad tempered witch doctor, a fizzy drink and your dad ?

A bottle of pop !

What do you get if
you cross a
pen with
Napoleon's feet ?

**A footnote
in history !**

What do you get if
you cross a skunk
and a pair of
rubber boots ?

Smelly wellies !

What do you get if you cross a ghost
and an Italian restaurant ?

Spookhetti !

What do you get if you cross a cow
with an out of date map ?

Udderly lost !

What do you get if you cross a
mad man and a bakery ?

Doughnuts !

What do you get if you cross a pelican and a zebra ?

Across the road safely !

What do you get if
you cross a bee
and a coach ?

A Buzzzz !

What do you get if
you cross a
monster and a
chicken ?

Free strange eggs !

What do you get if you cross a fish
and bad breath ?

Halibut - osis !

What do you get if you cross a
compass and a shellfish ?

A guided mussel !

What do you get if you cross a
skeleton and a garden spade ?

Skullduggery !

What do you get if you cross a school
with a computer supplier ?

Floppy desks !

What do you get if you cross a leopard
and a bunch of flowers ?

A beauty spot !

What do you get if you cross a biscuit with a car tyre ?

Crumbs !

What do you get if you cross a rabbit
and an aeroplane ?

The hare force !

What do you get if you cross a
Welshman with a problem ?

A Dai – lemma !

What do you get if you cross a pub and a steelworks ?

An iron bar !

What do you get if you cross a cow
and a jogging machine ?

A milk shake !

What do you get if you cross a book
and a pound of fat ?

Lard of the Rings !

What do you get if you cross teeth with candy ?

Dental floss !

What do you get if you cross a
newsreader and a toad ?

A Croaksman !

What do you get if you cross a
ghost and a newsreader ?

A Spooksman !

What do you get if you cross a
suitcase with a filbert ?

A nut case !

What do you get if you cross a radio music presenter
with Match of the Day ?

D D D D D D D D D D D D D D J !

What do you get if you cross a donkey
and Christmas ?

Muletide greetings !

What do you get if you cross the devil
and an anagram ?

Santa !

What do you get if you cross a Shakespeare
play and 3 eggs ?

Omelette !

What do you get if you cross a Shakespeare play
and a pig ?

A Ham omelette !

What do you get if you cross a Shakespeare
play and a vampire ?

Bat breath !

What do you get if you cross an
Eskimo and an ex-boyfriend ?

The cold shoulder !

What do you get if you cross a penguin and an elk ?

Chocolate moose !

What do you get if you cross a chemical and a bicycle ?

Bike carbonate of soda !

PECULIAR
PASTIMES...

It was a terrible tragedy, one of the world's finest
sprinters - died from pneumonia !

**Look on the bright side - at least his nose kept running
until the very end !**

What job does Dracula have with the
Transylvanian cricket team ?

He looks after the bats !

How can you describe cricket in three words ?

Rain Stopped Play !

What do you call the cat playing football ?

Puss In Boots !

SPORTING BOOKLIST

How to win at sport

by

Vic Tree

Horse training

by

Jim Kana

The cricketers' quiz book

by

R.U. Stumped

Why has the groundsman covered the grass in tar !?

Well - you told him to lay the pitch out for tonight's match !

My cousin has gold and silver medals in Karate, Cricket, Snooker, Horse Riding, High Jump, 200 Metres, Swimming, Marathon and Javelin !

Wow, he must be a super athlete !

No, he's a burglar actually !

What do you call a spooky cricketer ?

A wicked keeper !

What did it say on the snooker player's gravestone ?

Farewell to Jim, who has taken the long rest !

Ouch ! Why do you keep standing on my foot ?

Someone told me you were a stamp collector !

Did you ever play for the school football
team, Blenkinsop ?

I was left back, sir !
Left back in the changing rooms !

Why have you brought those cans of paint ?

Well, you said we were going trainspotting !

You played a magnificent innings - let me oil
your bat !

Why, I didn't hear it squeaking !

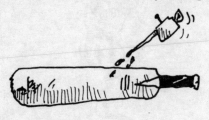

What game do elephants like playing with people ?

Squash !

What do you mean you don't like pop music ?

Well, would you listen to anything your father liked !

How long have you been interested in keeping goats ?

Ever since I was a kid !

HOBBIES BOOKSHOP

Butterflies of the world
by
Chris Aliss

Bird Watching
by
Haydn Seekum

Drawing and Painting
by
Art N Design

Stamp Collecting
by
Phil Attlee

Where do you put the lens cap when
you're taking pictures ?

On Len's head !

How are you getting on with your circuit training ?

Well, it's made me a lot fitter, but we haven't
done any electronics at all yet !

Why do you always paint rivers and
lakes in your pictures ?

Because I'm using water colours !

Why is it best to employ an alien
as a gardener ?

Because they have green fingers !

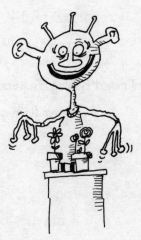

I didn't know your daughter
was interested in computer
games as well ?

**Yes, she's a microchip off the old
block !**

Why are you putting your wage packet in with the bread
mixture ?

I'm hoping it will give me a raise in pay !

That's amazing - whenever you ring a bell your dog runs
into the corner and sits down ?!

That's because he's a boxer !

Hoy, you can't fish here, this is a private lake !

I'm not fishing, I'm teaching my pet worm to swim !

These buns you've cooked taste of soap !

That's because they're Bath buns !

Why did you give up tap dancing then ?

I kept falling into the sink !

I think I'll take up jogging !

Well you had better start with your memory – because you forgot my birthday again !

ODDS AND ENDS

Did you hear about the monster who went
to a holiday camp?

He won the knobbly knees contest - with his face!

✎

What is dogma?

A female dog that's had puppies?"

✎

Are you really going to leave school at the end
of this term, Samantha,

or are you just saying it to cheer me up?"

✎

"Harry, why have you got a piano in the bathroom?"

"Because I'm playing chamber music!"

"Now I know there is a link between TV and violence !"

"How did you come to that conclusion ?"

"I told my teacher that I watched TV
instead of doing my
homework last night and she hit me !"

✎

What kind of jazz do witches like best ?

Hagtime !

✎

The water in our house is musical –

It's always piping hot !

✎

If you forget to do your homework for
our music teacher,

You'll soon find yourself in serious treble !

What is the easiest way to double your money ?

With a pair of scissors !

Why did the man walk around with his umbrella
open upside down ?

**He heard that there was going to be some
change in the weather !**

Why did the landlord of the pub have his
cash helmet on ?

In case anyone started throwing their money around !

What did the short sighted hedgehog
say to the cactus ?

"Ah, there you are dad !"

What do you call an insect at a sale ?

A Jumble Bee !

Why was the chef so relaxed ?

He had plenty of thyme on his hands !

What do you call a happy mushroom ?

Fun Gus !

What happened to the Scottish cat that ran into the road
without looking ?

It was kilt !

How long do you want your pyjamas ?

From about October to April !

What can be right but never wrong ?

The angles of a triangle !

What is the noisiest sport ?

Tennis - what a racket !

What is black and white and red in parts ?

A sunburnt penguin !

What animal wears a long coat in the Winter
and pants in the Summer ?

A dog !

There's no ham in this ham and mushroom pie !

And there's no cottage in the cottage pie either !

Why don't you go outside and play football
with your little brother ?

I'd rather use a proper football !

What do you get if you jump in the River Nile with bright
red swimming trunks on ?

Wet !

Roman soldier - "What's the time ?"

Another Roman soldier - "XVII past IX !"

How do ponies send secret messages ?

By horse code !

What sort of dog is used for sniffing out potatoes?

A spud hound!

Why do you call your dog camera?

Because it is always snapping at me!

What did the Eskimo girl do to get rid
of her boyfriend?

She gave him the cold shoulder!

What punishment do Eskimo children never have
to suffer at school?

Sitting in the corner!

Who held the baby octopus to ransom ?

Squidnappers !

What do you get if you cross a tin of baked
beans with a birthday cake ?

A cake that blows out its own candles !

What is goulash ?

A cremated ghost !

Who won the monster beauty contest ?

Nobody !

**My brother has a balanced diet –
he has a can of cola in each hand !**

Why are you wearing a wet shirt ?

Because the label says 'wash and wear' !

Why did the idiot make a hole in his umbrella ?

So that he could tell when it stopped raining !

Why are you home from school so early ?

I was sent home because my best friend was smoking !

But if your best friend was smoking –
why were YOU sent home ?

Because I was the one who set him on fire !

Can Steve come out to play ?

No, he's poorly in bed !

Well, can his cricket bat and ball come out to play ?

What game do monsters play at parties ?

Haunt the thimble !

What did the little monster say after he had been
eaten by the big monster ?

It's a little dark, but not as damp as my last flat !

Why did Manchester United want to sign Halley's Comet ?

Because they wanted a shooting star !

What does it mean if a monster's head lights up ?

That he's just had a bright idea !

What kind of coat will keep you warm in Winter?

A Blazer!

How do you spell mouse trap using only 3 letters?

C A T !

What did the postage stamp say to the envelope?

Stick with me and we'll go places!

I'd love to have your photo
And hang it in the shed
To frighten all the rats away
And scare the spiders dead.

Little Miss Muffet
Sat on her tuffet
Eating her kippers and spam
Along came a spider
And sat down beside her
So she ate that too, sprinkled with jam

A man was seen putting all the chairs from the
park into a lorry.

When someone asked him what he was
doing he replied...

"I'm making a band stand !"

FAMOUS LAST WORDS....

What does this button do ?

Of course it's not gas, pass me a match
and I'll show you !

There hasn't been a train along this line since 1965 !

Listen, I know poison when I taste it !

Of course I've taken the fuse out !

What did the monster have after his parents bought him a
saw for his birthday ?

Lots of half brothers and sisters !

Why are you hitting your head against the wall ?

**My hat is too large, so I'm trying to make
my head swell to fit !**

Is this the way to the railway station ?

You're certainly on the right track !

How long will the next train be ?

89 metres !

What do monsters do if they have naughty children
on their holiday flight ?

Put them outside to play !

What happened to the vampire
with bad breath ?

**His dentist told him to gargoyle
twice a day !**

Why should you not go down to the
woods today ?

Because it's the teddy scares picnic !

Where do aliens leave their spaceships ?

At a parking meteor !

A biology teacher from Leeds
Once swallowed a packet of seeds
A bright orange rose
Grew out of his nose
And his hair was a tangle of weeds !

Where do sharks come from?

Finland !

How does a snowman travel around ?

What was written on the robot's tombstone ?

Rust in pieces !

How does a snowman travel around ?

By icicle !

What is black, crazy and nests in a tree ?

A Raven lunatic !

Why is a bad golfer like an outboard motor ?

Because they both go putt, putt, putt, putt, putt....

What did the gun say to the bullet ?

You're fired, get out of here !

What do reindeer say before they start telling
you a joke ?

This one will sleigh you !

How did the snowman feel when he had a bad cold ?

Abominable !

Sardines really are the most stupid fish of all !

Why do you say that ?

**They lock themselves into little cans, and then
leave the key outside !**

What is black and white and can't turn round
in a narrow space ?

A nun carrying a snooker cue !

A man was shovelling snow from his front
pathway when a neighbour walked past.

"You're doing it the hard way, why not just
burn it away?"

The man thought long and hard about
this then replied,

**"But then I'd have to shovel all the
ashes away!"**

I think I've got chicken pox!

What makes you think it's chicken pox?

Because I feel peckish!

What do you get if you cross a
vampire and a jar of
peanut butter?

**A vampire that sticks to
the roof of your mouth!**

"Mummy, mummy, Charles has broken my favourite Doll !"

"How did he do that ?"

"When I hit him over the head with it !"

"When I grow up I want to be a ballet dancer !"

"That's a job that will keep you on your toes !"

"Dad, do you have a good memory for faces ?"

"I think so, son, why do you ask ?"

"Because I've just broken your shaving mirror !"

My dog loves to fly !

He's a jet setter !

✎

What did the old man do when he thought
he was dying ?

He moved his bed into the living room !

✎

"Please use the word 'information' in a sentence."

"Sometimes birds fly information !"

✎

"What makes you think I'm stupid ?"

**"Well, when you went to that mind reader she only charged
you half price !"**

✎

Which pets are the noisiest ?

Trumpets !

"I'd like two slices of steak, and make them lean!"

"Certainly, sir, which way?"

Did you hear about the man who thought the
Rover 3.5 was a robotic dog?

What happened to the robot who fell
off the fireplace?

He was dismantled!

What do you get if you cross a monster with a cat?

No more stray dogs for at least a 2 mile radius!

What is the difference between a burglar and a
man in a wig?

One has false keys, the other has false locks!

Where are famous monsters buried?

In Westmonster Cathedral!

✎

Your daughter has the ability to really go places
and, as her teacher, I can't wait!

✎

Our Art teacher draws her own conclusions!

✎

What trees are deck chairs made from?

Beach trees!

✎

How do skeletons listen to tapes?

On their bony walkmans!

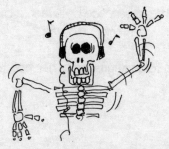

How can you tell that owls are wiser than chickens ?
Have you ever seen a Kentucky Fried Owl ?

What do you get if you travel in a space ship
with a toad ?

Star Warts !

Why did the man have a sausage stuck behind his ear ?

Because he'd just eaten his pencil !

When German cars retire
- do they go to the old Volks home ?

If Superman is so clever, why does he wear his
underpants on the outside of his trousers !

How can you tell when a train has just been past ?

They always leave tracks !

How can you tell if there's an elephant in the fridge?

You can't shut the door!

How do you communicate with a fish?

Drop it a line!

I used to be big headed - but now I'm perfect!

I never read books by Tolkien -

They are much too Hobbit forming!

You should never hit a man while he's down...

...he just might get up again and hit you back!

"Blenkinsop, why have you come to school
wearing only one glove?"

"The weather forecast said that on the one hand it might
be warm, but on the other hand it might be cool!"

Where do frogs and toads hang their coats?

In the croak room!

Why are brides so unlucky?

They never marry the best man!

Why should you never climb aboard an
alien space craft?

Because you might just get carried away!

What is white on the outside, black and green on
the inside and slippery when you eat it?

A slug and lettuce sandwich!

How do monsters get across the sea ?

On a cross channel furry !

✎

Why did the burglar saw the legs off his bed ?

Because he wanted to lie low for a while !

✎

"Waiter this omelette tastes awful !"

"Sir, I can assure you that our chef has been
making omelettes since he was a child !"

**"That may be true – but can I have one of his
fresher ones please ?"**

✎

What do you call a fat space alien ?

An Extra – cholesterol !

✎

What has four legs and flies ?

Two pairs of trousers !

I'm terribly homesick !

But this is your home !

I know, and I'm sick of it !

✎

I hear the monster executioner got a job in
a department store ?

Yes, he's now the Head Buyer !

✎

How can you tell when a mummy is angry ?

It flips its lid !

✎

Our needlecraft teacher is a real sew and sew !

What did the mummy burglar say when he was
found not guilty ?

"I beat the wrap !"

What do you call a hippo that wears flowers in its
hair and a string of beads around its neck ?

A Hippie - potamous !

Why did the stupid thief fly through the
jewellers shop window ?

He forgot to let go of the brick !

Why did the driver reverse up the motorway
in the wrong direction ?

Because he knew the rules of the road backwards !

What do you get if a cat sits on a beach at Christmas ?

Sandy claws !

A burglar tried to hold up a bank but found that he had brought his teddy bear instead of a gun.

What was he charged with ?

Assault with a teddly weapon !

What sort of glasses do ghosts wear ?

Spooktacles !

BATTY BOOKS - READ THEM NOW...

How to be a Great Gardener

By
Teresa Green

The Parachute Tester

By
Hugo Furst

Fishing From The Beach

By
C. Shaw

The Ghost Hunters

By
Terry Fied

Running A Guest House

By
Chris P Bacon

How To Make Your Own Desserts

By
I. Scream

A Holiday Abroad

By
Frances Close

My Criminal Life

By
Robin Banks

Living Life In The Nude

By
Major Stare

What do you know about the Dead Sea ?

I didn't even know it had been ill !

Do you always take a bath in such filthy water ?

It wasn't filthy when I got in !

Water - a colourless and odourless liquid,

that turns brown and smelly when I put my feet in it !

Two boys were fighting in the street. An old lady
separated them and gave them a telling off.

"You should learn a bit of give and take," she said.

"I have," replied one boy. "I gave him a thump
because he took my walkman !"

A bowl of lasagne walked into a pub and
ordered a drink.

"Sorry," said the barmaid, "we don't serve food
after 2 o'clock !"

What shall I do with all this soil I've got after
digging this hole ?

Just dig another hole and bury it !

What is black and white and black and white and black and
white and black and white and black and white and black
and white and black and white and black and white and
black and white and black and white and black and white
and black and white and black and white and black and
white and black and white and black and white and black
and white.....

A nun rolling down a hill !

Did you hear about the boy who thought
he was Dracula ?

He was a real pain in the neck !

Dad - there's a man here collecting for the
old folks home ?

Give him your Gran !

Which rich Arab invented crisps ?

Sultan Vinegar !

Who are the rudest creatures in the farmyard ?

Chickens - they are always using fowl language !

What do you call two spiders who have just
got married ?

Newly Webs !

Why did the monster stick a cartoonist up his nose when he
had a cold ?

Because toons help you breathe more easily !

Blenkinsop - I've told you before - stop acting
like an idiot !

But, sir, I'm not acting !

What do you get if a post office burns down?

Black mail !

Why do we have lips ?

To stop our mouths fraying at the edges !

This coffee is disgusting - it tastes like mud !

I'm not surprised - it was ground a few minutes ago !

My music teacher said I have a heavenly voice !

That's not strictly true - she said your voice was like nothing on Earth !

Last night someone made a hole in the fence
around the local nudist camp !

The local police are looking into it round the clock !

Did you hear about the idiot who invented a
new spray to kill garden insects ?

**You spray it on all your plants - it kills them all
stone dead - so the insects starve !**

Where do nudist comedians get all their jokes ?

They employ stripped writers !

Blenkinsop - you weren't in school last Friday,
and I understand from some of your classmates
that you were, in fact, at a disco !

**That's not true, Miss, and I still have the cinema
tickets to prove it !**

Did you hear about the man who decided to
complain about the food in a Chinese restaurant.
He called over the waiter...

"That steak was rubbery !"

**"Thank you for the compliment, sir, and have a
rubbery evening !"**

Did you hear about the idiot who wrote himself
a letter, forgot to sign it and then, when it arrived, couldn't
work out who it was from !

Darling - your cheeks are like petals - bicycle petals...

Your teeth are like stars - they come out at night...

Your skin is like a million dollars - all green and crinkly !

Which ghost haunts the 3 bears ?

Ghouldilocks !

What is the capital of Australia?

A!

Why was the little girl wrapped up in bandages?

Because she was mummy's little pet!

How do you know when a cannibal fancies
eating you?

He keeps buttering you up!

What sort of wine do cannibals like best?

One with plenty of body in it!

Can I share your skis?

Sure – you have them going uphill, and I'll have
them going down!

What lives in a forest and tells the dullest stories
ever heard ?

A wild boar !

How does Frankenstein's monster sit in a chair ?

Bolt upright !

What did the giant spider from outer space build ?

A World Wide Web !

What do you say when you meet a toad ?

Wart's new with you !?

What sort of bull doesn't have horns ?

A Bullfrog !

Which fish can only be seen at night ?

A Starfish !

Which TV station do werewolves watch ?

Channel Fur !

Where is the only place on Earth where Friday
comes before Thursday ?

A Dictionary !

What do you call a witch flying through the skies ?

Broom Hilda !

What sort of can can you set light to ?

A candle !

Why did the body builder rub grease onto his muscles at bedtime ?

He needed to be oily the next morning !

That good looking boy over there is getting on my nerves !

But he's not even looking at you ?

That's what is getting on my nerves !

Teacher - I hope I didn't see you cheating then, Blenkinsop !

Blenkinsop - I hope you didn't see me cheating either, Miss !

Did you hear about the meanest man in the world?

...He found a pair of crutches on a train, and went home and broke his brother's leg!

...When I saw him stripping the wallpaper in his house I said I didn't know he was redecorating –
He said he wasn't redecorating
– he was moving house!

...he took up passive smoking to save money!

...he pinched this book from a friend instead of buying his own copy!

ANIMAL FARM

On Christmas Eve a married couple were looking up into the sky at something travelling towards them.

Is it a snow storm? asked the wife

No, it looks like reindeer, replied the husband!

✎

What do you do if an elephant sits in front of you at the cinema?

Miss the film!

✎

What did the Pink Panther say when he stood on an ant?

Dead ant, dead ant, dead ant dead ant dead ant...

✎

What do elephants take to help them sleep?

Trunkquilisers!

What did the dog say when it sat on some sandpaper ?

Ruff !

What do you call a delinquent octopus ?

A crazy, mixed -up squid !

What is the most cowardly farmyard creature ?

The Chicken !

What is the tallest yellow flower in the World ?

A Giraffodil !

What is the cheapest way to hire a horse?

Stand it on four bricks!

What sort of bird steals from banks?

A Robin!

What is green and white and hops?

An escaping frog sandwich!

What do you call a stupid elephant with his
own aeroplane?

A Dumbo Jet!

What do you call a large grey animal that's
just eaten a ton of beans ?

A smellyphant !

Mary had a little lamb
the lamb began to tease her
'Stop it', she said,; the lamb refused
and now it's in the freezer !

BRRRR...

When Mary had a little lamb
the doctor was surprised
but when old MacDonald had a farm
he couldn't believe his eyes !

Why did the chicken blush ?

Because it saw the salad dressing !

What sort of animal does a ghost ride ?

A night mare !

How do ducks play tennis ?

With a quacket !

Why is an elephant like a teacher ?

**Put a tack on an elephants chair
and you'll soon find out !**

What is big and grey and good at sums ?

An elephant with a calculator !

What do you get if you cross a hunting dog with a newspaper writer ?

A newshound !

Why do bears have fur coats ?

Because they can't get plastic macs in their size !

Where is the hottest place in the jungle ?

Under a gorilla !

Two cows were talking in a field....

First Cow - Are you worried about catching this mad cow disease ?

Second Cow - Baaaa !

Why did the chicken run out onto the football pitch ?

Because the referee whistled for a fowl !

Where do horses sit when they go to the theatre?

In the stalls!

Why did the chicken cross the playground?

To get to the other slide!

What ballet stars pigs?

Swine Lake!

What do you do with a green elephant?

Wait until he's ripe!

Which is the trendy horse ?

The one with the pony tail !

What says Moo, Baaa, Woof, Quack, Meeoooow, Oink ?

A sheep that speaks foreign languages !

Which animals with a cold do the police use ?

Sniffer dogs !

Where would you find an alien
milking a cow ?

In the milky way !

Where do rabbits learn to fly helicopters ?

In the hare force !

What is the best way to get in touch with a fish ?

Drop him a line !

Good morning Mr Butcher - do you have pigs' trotters ?

No, I always walk like this !

What do you get if you cross a pig with a millipede ?

Bacon with legs !

Why can't I get the King of the jungle
on the telephone ?

Because the lion is busy !

What was the name of the woman who crossed the
Gobi desert on a dromedary ?

Rhoda Camel !

Why does a Flamingo lift up one leg ?

Because if it lifted them both up it would fall down !

Where would you hear fowl language on a farm ?

Outside the chicken coop !

My mum and dad said my new boyfriend isn't fit
to live with pigs !

What did you say to that ?

I stuck up for him, I said of course he is !

Why do elephants have trunks ?

**Because they would never fit their huge
clothes into a suitcase !**

When do lions have twelve feet ?

When there are three of them !

First leopard – Hey, is that a
jogger over there ?

**Second leopard – Yes, great,
I love fast food !**

Johnny – Mum, is our dog metric ?

Mum – Why do you ask ?

**Johnny – Because Dad said
it has just had a
litre of puppies ?!**

What is round, brown, smelly and
plays music ?

A cowpat on a record player !

What is black and white and gets
complaints from all the neighbours?

A zebra learning to play the drums!

How can you get eggs without chickens?

By keeping geese and ducks!

Why should you be naughty if you have
a cow for a teacher?

**Because if you are good you might
get a pat on the head!**

What is the first thing Tarzan puts on in the morning ?

His jungle pants !

Where do cows go for their holidays ?

Moo York

or

Patagonia

or

Uddersfield !

What grows down as it grows up ?

A Goose !

How do you stop a skunk from smelling ?

Tie a knot in his nose !

What is it called when a cat falls from the farmhouse roof and smashes all the glass in the greenhouse ?

A Catastrophe !

First goldfish - I told you we'd be famous one day - and now it's going to come true !

Second goldfish - Wow! When is all this going to happen ?

First goldfish - They're putting us on the television tomorrow !

Where do farm animals keep their savings ?

In a Piggy bank !

What do you call an insect that has
forgotten the words?

A Humbug!

What do pussy cats read with their mice crispies?

Mewspapers!

What game do skunks play?

Ping Pong!

How do frogs send messages to each other?

Morse Toad!

What do cows eat for breakfast ?

Moosli !

Why are cows rubbish at maths ?

Because they haven't invented the cowculator yet !

What television channel do wasps watch ?

The Beee Beee Ceee !

Why do some animals wear cowboy boots in the jungle ?

Because they go lion dancing !

Where are all the aspirins in the jungle?

There aren't any - the paracetamol!

What was the 30 metre tall Monopoly box
doing in the jungle?

It was a big game hunter!

What do country and western singers
wear in the jungle?

Rhino-stones!

Why don't leopards bother to cheat in exams?

Because they know that they will always be spotted!

Why was the zebra put in charge of the jungle army ?

Because he had the most stripes !

What is smelly and has no sense of humour ?

A dead hyena !

What do you call a well dressed jungle cat ?

A dandy lion !

Where do horses stay on their honeymoon ?

In the bridle suite !

What is cold, furry and minty?

A Polo Bear!

✐

Where would you find a 10,000 year old cow?

In a Moooseum!

✐

What sort of sheep stick to the bottom of boats?

Baaaaanacles!

✐

As sheep don't have money, how do they buy and sell?

They have a baaarter system!

Why did the sheep buy a hotel?

He's always wanted to own a baaa!

Whal sweet thing do sheep like best?

Chocolate baaaaars!

What do cows put on in the morning?

Udder pants!

How do you control a horse?

Bit by bit!

Why was the young horse sent out of the classroom ?

He was acting the foal !

Doctor, doctor, I'm turning into a young cat !

You must be kitten me !

Why do cats always finish the job ?

Because they purr - severe !

Where do cats go when they die ?

The Purrr - ly gates !

Where do rodents go for holidays ?

Hamster Dam !

✏

What sort of jokes do chickens like best ?

Corny ones !

(which is why we sell so many copies
of this book to chickens !)

✏

What was the name of the horse that
fought windmills ?

Donkey Oatey !

✏

How can you travel through the jungle at
60 miles an hour ?

Inside a cheetah !